FORESIGHT

UNFOLDING THE
PLOT OF THE BIBLE

- To establish a close vital relationship with God

- To identify with Christ's operation to save the lost and conquer the kingdom of the world

LARRY GRABILL

Copyright @ Larry Grabill, 2020

All rights reserved. No portion of this book may be reproduced in any form or by any electronic or mechanical means, including information storage and retrieval systems, without express permission from the author, except in the case of brief quotations embodied in critical articles and reviews.

Published in the United States of America.

www.larrygrabill.com

Larry Grabill

Foresight: Unfolding the Plot of the Bible

1st edition, Sept, 2020

ISBN: 978-0-9717235-3-5

PRINTED IN THE UNITED STATES OF AMERICA

Cover design, book design/layout by Larry Grabill.

Unless otherwise noted, all Scripture quotations from are from the ESV® Bible (The Holy Bible, English Standard Version®), copyright© 2001 by Crossway Bibles, a publishing ministry of Good News Publishers. Used by permission. All rights reserved.

Contents

Chapter 1
Perversion 3

Chapter 2
The Remnant Established 7

Chapter 3
A New Start 15

Chapter 4
Secular Humanism Introduced 33

Chapter 5
Systematic Idolatry Invented 39

Chapter 6
Called Out 47

Chapter 7
The Test 57

Chapter 8
The Self-Centered Path 67

Chapter 9
Full Surrender 73

Chapter 10
Delivered 81

Chapter 11
The Ten Commandments 89

Conquering the Promised Land..95

Chapter 13
Earthly Kingdom Inaugurated 101

Chapter 14
A Man After God's Own Heart 105

Chapter 15
Seventy Years..113

Chapter 16
End of the Seventy Years 117

Chapter 17
Seventy Weeks of Years...123

Chapter 18
Zechariah's Visions...131

Chapter 19
The Little Horn 139

Chapter 20
The Kingdom of God at Hand...151

Chapter 21
Passover to the Lord's Supper 179

Chapter 22
The Hellish Plot 191

Chapter 23
World Crisis...195

Chapter 24
Resurrection and Ascension...211

Holy Spirit Baptism 217

Chapter 26

Apostle Paul and Aristarchus 233

Chapter 27

Apostle John and Gaius 241

Chapter 28

Conquest.. 247

Introduction

This book creates a realistic, imaginary narrative to unfold the Bible's plot to save the lost and conquer the kingdom of the world. As the story progresses it incorporates many quotes from Scripture. In harmony with these quotes the story portrays pictures of various themes threaded through the Bible. And these pictures gradually unfold the plot. In this way a Bible study develops which reads like a novel.

Larry Grabill

Foresight

Chapter 1

Perversion

Breathlessly, he waited in the cover of the beautiful foliage. The woman cautiously approached. Her eyes were fixed on the luscious fruit hanging from the branches.

"Good day, Madam Eve."

"Oh, you startled me!" gasped Eve. "What are you doing here?"

"I have to confess, I'm not really sure. I felt destiny calling me. But what a fantastic privilege to be in your beautiful presence," replied the serpent.

"Oh, thank you. I'm flattered. But I really shouldn't be here. God instructed Adam and me not to eat of this tree lest we die."

"Bah. This tree and its fruit are perfectly harmless. You will not die. Everything God made is good for us to eat."

"Mmmm. You are so charming and reassuring, but I am still afraid to eat of this tree, Mr. Serpent. Adam and I have a *covenant* with the Lord. It confers eternal life and his blessing on us as long as we obey him."

"Now listen. You really should understand something that God doesn't want you to know. This tree holds the key to a great new lease on life for you. If you eat of it, you will no longer be dependent on God for guidance. You will have full knowledge of what is good for

Foresight

you without having to depend on God's revelation."

"That really would be wonderful, but I have been in the habit of *believing* God's word. Doesn't it show me what is good for me and what is harmful to me / what is good and what is evil?"

"Oh Eve, your manner of speech is so enthralling that I hate to suggest your thoughts are not profound. But my affection for you compels me to inform you that such God-thinking is naïve. Expand your horizons. Rely more on your own understanding. When you discover how delicious the fruit of this tree is, you will know that God was just trying to keep you from loving it so you would not be distracted from *loving* Him. Now feast your eyes on that fruit and you will soon know that your *hope* lies in it."

"Hum. Mr. Serpent, you are so enchanting and liberating. And now that I engage the full powers of my mind, I discover that it is right to determine what I should *love* by what might satisfy my physical appetite. I also see that I should decide where to place my *hope* by what appeals to my eyes...."

"Yes. Yes. And what is more important than living for self-gratification and the possession of material things?" suggested Satan. "Mr. Serpent, thanks to you, I am completely captivated by the realization that I can discover what my needs are on my own, apart from *faith* in God. Yes. Yes. I will partake. I will *trust* my own judgment and be proud of it. Mmmm.....This fruit is so good. It is the most delicious food I have ever tasted."

"Eve!" cried Adam.

Startled, Eve turned to see the anguished look on Adam's face.

"What are you doing? That fruit is forbidden. Oh, no! You are going to die."

Eve froze. Then her gaze snapped back in the direction of the serpent, but he was gone. Her jaw dropped. Slowly comprehension began to dawn. Fear crept into her soul as the hypnotic spell abated.

"My God. What have I done?" she whispered.

Perversion

Husband and wife stared past each other for a long time. Then cautiously Eve turned her eyes to Adam's face. He sensed she was looking but continued to stare past her for some time. Finally, he shifted his eyes to meet her solicitous gaze.

The garden was still and quiet.

The rippling nearby stream stopped its flow.

The animals held their breath.

The sky became an eerie gray.

The hard lines on Adam's face gradually softened. He bowed his head, cupped his hands over his head, and drew in a deep breath. Then releasing the air from his lungs, he lifted his head and reached for his wife. "I am so sorry. I should have insisted on going with you today."

"The serpent deceived me. He convinced me that eating the fruit would make me wise."

"Eve my dear, if only I had been with you. Together we would have overcome. I can't bear to have you die and leave me alone."

"I am so afraid," sobbed Eve. "Please partake of the fruit so that we may be together in whatever awaits me."

"How dare I? If I eat from the tree, I will separate myself from God. Yet if I don't eat, I will no longer be at one with you." Sweat broke from Adam's brow. He doubled over and slumped to the ground. His body shook and trembled.

Eve turned away with a hollow stare into the darkening sky.

Gradually Adam gained control. "I must take responsibility for your action and act with you." He reached for the remainder of the fruit in Eve's hand. "I am fully aware that something called death will result from this."

"Eve, my dear, we will no longer eat of the Tree of Life, the most important tree of the garden. And I am not sure what the death we have incurred will deliver, having never seen it. But I am sure that you like me feel deep *despair* because of our actions. This *despair* tells me our *hope* in God is greatly diminished. How can we ever have

Foresight

a close relationship with God again, even if God should find a way to redeem us?

Chapter 2

The Remnant Established

Gabriel hovered above the crystal glass sea before the throne of God. A shining beam of heavenly light refracted through the sea into beautiful hues across his garment. On his shoulder he bore the winged, gold emblem signifying his status as messenger angel. He had ascended here from his ministry on earth. Michael stood directly below him on the sea. The heavenly light emblazoned him with even more of the prism effect of the crystal glass sea, refracting the gorgeous hues across his being. The emblem signifying his rank as archangel shimmered blue, purple, and scarlet colors from his left shoulder.

"Satan's campaign is in full swing," said Gabriel. "He continues the same strategy he used with Eve. He deceives society into *loving* what gives instant sensory gratification instead of *loving* God. He entices people to place their *hope* in the material world which appeals to the eyes instead of valuing the spiritual and eternal. Furthermore, he teaches them to rely on their own judgment at the expense of placing *faith* in God's revelation."

"People's capacity for love is thus perverted into *sensualism*, their capacity for hope into *materialism,* and their capacity for faith into *humanism*. These three -isms turn people from worshiping the Almighty and fellowshipping with him to worshiping themselves. They live just to pleasure their senses instead living in the joy of the Lord through prayer and fellowship with their Maker. They are perversions that cry, 'Liberate yourself from servile obedience to the Lord! Do your own thing. Live your own life.' People fall for this appeal to their egos and slip right into the clutches of Satan."

"Adam and Eve were in dominion over the animal world including their own animalistic, bodily senses and cravings. But now their physical senses and cravings dominate them. This carries through to their descendants. It causes all kinds of perversions. Hatred, anger, lust, and envy consume them until they destroy each other and drive themselves to *despair*. Satan banks on this *despair* having the power to keep them from ever contemplating having the winning, hopeful, abundant life God gives."

Michael's countenance continued to darken while Gabriel told him all this, but then his face brightened. "There is one who does not fall for Satan's scam. His name is Abel. I have been marshaling the angels to minister to his spirit. It is really refreshing to see him taking God's way and avoiding all the other deviant paths. He is deeply in love with God and doesn't let the self-indulgent, hateful crowd deter him in any way."

* * *

Meanwhile Satan was having a meeting with his imps. His gleaming eyes pierced through squinting, black eyelids as he boasted, "We are making great headway, my evil, conniving imps. I must congratulate you on your very effective work. Of course, I was the one who discovered the winning strategy to poke the apple of God's eye. Yes I, the most brilliant strategist of all times, discovered how to pry people away from God. I first struck at people's capacity for *love*. I convinced Eve to determine what she should *love* by what gratified her physical appetite. (Then her heart opened to determine in what she should *hope* by what appealed to her eye.) This then incentivized her to pridefully place *faith* in her own judgment and ignore God's warning. God has put it this way:

> When the woman saw that the tree was good for food, and that it was a delight to the eyes, and that the tree was to be desired to make one wise (Genesis 3:6).

This must mean that Eve *loved* what gratified her appetite, *hoped* in what delighted her eyes, and pridefully placed *faith* in her own understanding.

"Now listen up, my wicked friends. Abel is setting a course to turn society back to God. He loves God so much he is determined have fellowship with him and do right. He has learned from his parents' mistake. He refuses to even give me an audience. How rude. But Cain.... Cain is a different story. We can use him to destroy Abel's good influence on society. We have inspired Cain to obsessively focus his capacity for *love* on the sensory, satisfying his physical appetite on the fruit of his garden. This is similar to what I did with Eve. He grows and nurtures his garden into beautiful vegetables in spite of the curse of weeds. And the really good part is he *pridefully* puts his *faith* in his gardening. He fully depends on it, the work of his own hands, to sustain him instead depending on God. He places his *hope* in the plants and the material things of life. Yes, he is going down the same path his mama did. Only, our grip on him is much stronger. I could only deceive Eve for a few minutes, but Cain is immersed in my deception," continued the evil one.

"The next step will be easy for us. Being devoid of godly love, Cain's heart is wide open to receiving hatred. So I am counting on

Foresight

you imps who specialize in hate to fill him with hateful rage and direct it at Abel. Drive him mad with anger until he determines to do something drastic. Do you understand?"

"Yes!" the devilish imps cried. One imp bared his teeth and spat. "We are at your service, most ugly, deceiving Master. You deceived us into following you and rejecting God. Now we have no choice but to try to destroy God's causes in hope of gaining satisfaction and revenge on Him. But really we should be taking revenge on you."

"Shut up. And get to work lest I banish you from working with us."

* * *

Cain clenched his teeth in rage as he glared at Abel whose face glowed with the joy of the Lord. The iron claws of hateful anger sank deeper and deeper into Cain's soul with a crushing grip. The pressure made his spirit cry, "Kill him! Kill him! He has no right to be exuberant in his *love* for God when he sees God rejecting your sacrifice. Your brother should identify with your anger at being rejected, even though God accepted his sacrifice."

> The Lord said to Cain, "Why are you angry, and why has your face fallen? If you do well, will you not be accepted? And if you do not do well, sin is crouching at the door. Its desire is contrary to you, but you must rule over it" (Genesis 4:6-7).

Cain walked away muttering to himself, "No. I am not going to go crawling to my brother and ask him for one of his lambs. I am not going to sacrifice to a God who has shown disgusting partiality to him. The Lord should have accepted my sacrifice of garden plants because they were the best I had to offer. They reflected who I am as a gardener. Abel offered the lamb to represent himself as a shepherd and the Lord accepted it. God is prejudiced against anyone who is not a shepherd. I have a right to be extremely angry."

The Remnant Established

Abel pursued his brother, calling, "Cain. I will be glad to give you a lamb. Please come back and do the right thing."

The iron claws jabbed deeper, "Oh, that self-righteous saint. How insulting can he be? Yes, he is happy to exalt himself even more with his faux generosity. He is not fit to live. He must go down."

Cain fled to the cover of the trees ahead. He had to be alone to process. Walking deep into the forest, he finally fell to the ground exhausted. Night brought no relief. The anger persisted through broken sleep. Early in the morning he trudged home, his devilish determination mounting with each step.

When he found Abel, he said, "Let's go for a walk and talk things over."

Abel gladly obliged, anxious to be reconciled. They walked for a mile in silence, "What do you want to say to me, brother?" Abel finally asked.

Those were to be his last words. Cain exploded into action and the dastardly deed was done. He covered the body with brush and leaves and returned to his garden.

> Then the Lord said to Cain, "Where is Abel your brother?" He said, "I do not know; am I my brother's keeper?" And the Lord said, "What have you done? The voice of your brother's blood is crying to me from the ground. And now you are cursed from the ground, which has opened its mouth to receive your brother's blood from your hand. When you work the ground, it shall no longer yield to you its strength. You shall be a fugitive and a wanderer on the earth." Cain said to the Lord, "My punishment is greater than I can bear" (Genesis 4:9-13).

* * *

"The wickedness will not stop with Cain. The self-centered quest for dominance will continue," declared Gabriel. People fail to realize

Foresight

that the selfishness of it all leads to unhealthy competition, jealousy, and hatred. Violence will follow and society will progress towards *despair*."

"The thought of what God is going to have to do to stop people from destroying everything good and annihilating themselves in the process is truly scary," replied Michael. "It obviously will be something drastic. Society is in for a rude awakening."

Gabriel stared off into the distance. "In spite of all this I have hope. I heard God has a plan to save mankind from the wicked strategies of the evil one. Someday people will be able to eat again from the Tree of Life. This is the only information being released. The details are top secret, classified information. The purpose of the secrecy is to keep Satan off balance."

"I can understand why. What I don't understand is why the ole devil was allowed to know so much about people, like the fact they have the power to disobey God if they choose. Seems Satan would not have tried to trick Adam and Eve into eating of the forbidden fruit if he had not known this. Anyway, the details of the top-secret plan are not available to us angels under your rank. Maybe you are authorized to have this intelligence, but not me."

"I know little, but I do have a clue. I have been keeping my ear tuned to hear what the Lord says. I heard him say to the serpent after the serpent corrupted Adam and Eve:

> He shall bruise your head, and you shall bruise his heel" (Genesis 3:15).

Obviously, this has come to pass. People have hostility toward snakes and often are inclined to land a blow on their heads. And snakes bite people, often on the heel. But I have a feeling there is more to the prophecy than just this obvious fulfillment. I believe God intends to judge Satan (bruise his head) for the sin he has brought to people (bruising their heels) to save them from the effects of sin."

"Well Michael, we know God offers to forgive people when they offer animal sacrifices in faith for salvation. Abel took advantage of his provision and is eternally saved in the afterlife. Satan prompted Cain to kill him, but now Abel lives."

"Yes. His spirit lives in Sheol but it is confined there, and his body lies in the ground. I am sure God has something better in store. An animal's life is sacrificed for the sin. The idea is that sin brings death. The animal must die and shed his blood vicariously for sinners to allow them to go free. But the blood and the death of the animal sacrificed is only a token of what it will take to atone for sin. Sin is much more serious than the death of animals so their blood cannot take away sin."[1]

"Maybe God has a plan to sufficiently atone for sin, so people won't have to spend eternity apart from God."

Gabriel's eyes lit up as he listened, "Michael, I believe you might have stumbled onto some top secret, classified intelligence."

"Yes. Yes. I believe you're right. We won't breathe a word to anyone. Not even to the other angels. We must keep Satan in the dark. In the meantime, God has begun to establish a faith-path of godliness for people to follow through the examples of a *remnant* who follow him. Abel's example is the beginning of that path. "Biblical history will record:

> "By faith Abel offered to God a more acceptable sacrifice than Cain, through which he was commended as righteous, God commending him by accepting his gifts. And through his faith, though he died, he still speaks" (Hebrews 11:4).

Michael continued, "A man who came after him named Enoch faithfully walked with God. Biblical history will say of Enoch:

> "By faith Enoch was taken up so that he should not see death, and he was not found, because God had taken him. Now before he was taken he was commended as having pleased God" (Hebrews 11:5).

Gabriel took notice, "As you have pointed out, Michael, God has

---

[1] See Hebrews 10:4

Foresight

begun to build his faith-path for people to follow through his *remnant* of people like Abel and Enoch. Abel recognized his need of a blood sacrifice to atone for his sins. Enoch followed the same course and gained the reputation of living to please God. Yes, the *remnant* is established in these two and others who follow the faith-path with them.

Chapter 3

A New Start

"Noah. I am the Lord God Almighty. Listen to Me. The world has become corrupt. You and your family are the only ones on the face of the earth who live by the truth and follow me. Others try to convince themselves that anything they want to do is good. They lie, cheat, steal, murder, and corrupt themselves with many perversions and evil deeds. I will destroy the world before it destroys your descendants and leaves the world with none righteous who believe and hope in me.

"You must build a huge wooden ship 500 ft. long, 83 ft. wide, and 50 ft. high. It shall have three decks with space for ventilation between the top of the walls and the roof. You, your family, and two of each common animal species—plus seven of every clean animal—will go into that ark. There will be room in it for all of you and the food you will need. I will bring a worldwide flood to destroy all living beings on the earth. But you will rise above it all and be safe." God paused, waiting for Noah to catch up and understand.

"Really? A flood that will cover the whole earth? I certainly want

Foresight

to be saved from that. A deluge of that magnitude is an awesome, scary thought. But build a ship 500 ft. long? I am not sure I am up to the task." Noah questioned.

"Have I not helped you do everything else I called you to do?"

"Yes, but I am afraid people will laugh me to scorn if I attempt this."

"Which are you more afraid of, people laughing at you, or the flood that I assure you is coming?"

"Alright Lord, You win. I will trust you to help me undertake this humongous task. Wow! Who ever heard of a ship 500 ft. long? Yes Lord, I will need a huge amount of your amazing grace to build such a vessel. But Lord, are you not being too rash? Will you not give my neighbors a chance to repent? Some of them might turn to you if we warn them of what is to come."

"Not only will they have a chance to repent. The ark will be an object lesson of warning rising before their very eyes. They will have 120 years to consider turning from their evil ways. I am a merciful and longsuffering God."

"You are saying that I will be able to build the ark in 120 years? That will take some doing."

"Yes. The flood will come in 120 years. You have no time to waste," declared the Lord.

~

"Shem, my son and able foreman of Noah's Boat Construction Company, I have something to tell you. We have been given a contract to build a ship five times bigger than anyone has ever built."

"And would you mind telling me who gave us this contract?" Shem asked.

"None other than God Almighty," Noah answered.

"My honorable father, whom I highly respect. Let me ask. Are you sure you heard correctly?" inquired Shem.

A New Start

Noah stared at his son, and Shem nodded.

"Alright, I see you are convinced. And I know that once you've made up your mind, nothing can divert you from your purpose."

"Yes son, the ship architect will soon have the plans ready and he will thoroughly brief you on how to proceed. In the meantime, you can assure all the workers they will have work for a long, long time."

"May I ask you why God wants us to build such a monstrous ship?" Shem asked.

"God said a worldwide flood is coming to destroy the world. We will need a big boat for us and all the animals God will bring into the ark."

"Oh. Oh. Oh." said Shem.

~

"Brother Ham," said Japheth, "I hope you appreciate all the materials my crew is supplying your inventory. It takes a lot of hard work to fell trees, saw boards, and laminate those massive beams."

"Of course I appreciate your work. But you are not the only one who works around here. I work from sunup to sundown identifying each piece of timber and noting where to place it. If I didn't do this the builders would have mass confusion." Ham declared.

"Oh your work is easy. You just shuffle papers. I am in charge of the real work. I even do a lot of the chopping and sawing myself. Look at that muscle," Japheth said, curling his arm to bulge his muscle.

"Oh yah? You always think you work harder than me. It takes brains to do my work—a whole lot more than it takes for yours. Father knows where to put the man with the real head on his shoulders. And don't think for a moment that my work is not real work. I go to bed exhausted every night," Ham argued.

"Yah. Yah. I hear you. It is good your work doesn't take muscles. Let me feel if you have any muscle there. Is that a bicep?"

Foresight

"Ouch, you big ox." Ham pushed him away.

Japheth laughed uproariously.

Just then Shem arrived on the scene. "What are you guys carrying on about?"

"Awe, Japheth thinks he is the only one that works around here."

"Oh for goodness sake. You surely don't believe that do you, Japheth?" Shem quizzed.

"I am simply saying that real work is using your muscles. Ham only works his brains and he thinks that is real work."

Shem smirked, "Both of you have it easy compared to my work. Don't forget, I am in charge of building the ship. It takes both brains, and muscles, to do my work. I have to keep everybody working together in harmony and make sure the work is done right. One has to know how to motivate people and organize their efforts. I also lend a hand where heavy lifting is required." He wrapped his big arms around Japheth's and Ham's necks and bumped their heads together.

"Yoow!" the brothers cried.

"Now quarreling brothers, let's all get back to work. We only have fifty more years to complete the ark," instructed Shem.

~

"I have to admit Noah is quite the engineer to be able to design and build this huge boat, but where is the water? Does Noah plan to transport his ship to the sea?" suggested Mr. Skeptic.

"Noah preaches that God will send a massive flood to cover the whole earth. The water will come to his boat, instead of his boat to water," replied Mr. Frivolous.

"Ha ha ha. Ha ha ha. Ha ha ha. You can't be serious. How does Noah think he can know the mind of God? Why would God want to send a flood?"

"He says God will send a flood to cover the earth and destroy all flesh because we are so corrupt."

A New Start

"Ha ha ha. So we have a moralist on our hands. I suppose Noah thinks he will scare everyone into his ark. Ha ha ha. Ha ha ha."

Lady Promiscuous chimed in, "Noah should know that we are all habitual sinners by nature and cannot expect to be different. God only wants us to look to him for forgiveness. He doesn't expect us to live good moral lives. Besides He is too loving to destroy His children. Noah is only a shipbuilder. What does he know? He should leave the preaching to the learned who are not so rash."

Atheist bristled, "You all are full of nonsense. God doesn't even exist. We don't have to account to any supreme being as though he created us. The world came into being by spontaneous generation. You all need to get liberated from your crazy ideas. All this talk of God is what gives us crackpots like Noah. I won't give his rantings a second thought."

~

The sweat rolled down Shem's brawny face as he approached Noah, "Father, you say God wants to destroy the world to preserve knowledge of the truth and keep society from destroying itself. I don't quite understand."

Noah brushed his hand down over his dusty beard and replied, "People who love God, and the truth he promotes, are conscious of the consequences of their actions. But when they turn from God they get confused about the truth and lose hold on reality. Then they actually become convinced that their selfish acts of lying, cheating, sexual immorality, dishonest politics, and fraudulent business dealings have good consequences. They are not guided by love-principles established in *God's Word* to provide the foundation for a healthy society. No wonder their world becomes dysfunctional."

"God intends to destroy the world because he wants to preserve society?" queried Ham with a mystified look.

"That's right, Ham. Even though destroying most of the world

Foresight

will be drastic action, it'll keep society from totally annihilating itself. We who are willing to live by the truth will have a chance to repopulate the earth."

Japheth appeared from around the bow of the ark, wiping his sweaty brow with a gray cloth, "Do you think anyone will enter the ark with us when it is time go in?"

"I don't know," sighed Noah. "But we know what is coming so we must trust God to enable us to build the ark."

"What about the animals, Father? How will we roundup all the animals and get them in the ark?"

"Only God knows, Ham, but remember animals normally have a sense of any impending disaster. They may come out of natural instinct or they may come by the Lord's direct control. But they will come when the ship is ready."

~

Standing before the ark with the wind bristling their hair, Shem and Noah surveyed the progress. Shem spoke, "It is so awesome to see how God provides the materials, wisdom, and strength to build his ark of deliverance. Our laborers have never worked so efficiently in providing timbers from the forest. The saw men have never produced such excellent lumber. The carpenters work with passion and take extreme pride in fastening the beams and planks together with tightly fit joints. I am confident our ship will be strong enough to survive any rough waters she will be called upon to sail."

"Do you think the ark can be finished in ten more years?" asked Noah.

"We only have ten more years?"

"That's right. In ten years the flood is coming."

"This is going to be tough. Father, you need to pray for us. We haven't even started the roof yet nor any of the pitching on the outside of this monstrosity. The sea anchors have to be made and many of the cages have yet to be constructed."

~

Noah turned from inspecting the great ship and exited its only door. Walking down the gangplank, he lifted his suntanned face and brown eyes to heaven. He stretched out his hands with palms turned upward. "Lord, your ark is all pitched and ready. The cages are in place. The drift anchors are tied to the stern with huge long ropes. My family's energy is spent, and we still have to get all those animals in the boat."

"Don't worry, I will renew your strength. As you know, none have turned from their self-centered corruption and agreed to enter the ark with your family at the appointed time, so you will need extra strength to carry on the duties awaiting you in the ark."

"I am sorry, Lord, I have preached my heart out to everyone and done my best to convince them that you are serious. But no one listens. I feel like a failure."

"Be encouraged Noah. Your sons, their wives, and your wife are still faithful."

"Yes indeed, Lord. We know that your way is the only way to have abundant life. Furthermore, we fear to displease you. We know that we would die in the coming flood if we should depart from the path of righteousness. But we realize that we have nothing to fear as we walk in your ways, You Oh Lord are faithful and true. We love you with all of our hearts."

"Then you are not a failure, Noah. You have saved your family from the self-centered corruption of others that seeks to impose itself on you at your every turn. You have labored hard and have finished the ark in a mere 120 years in the face of all kinds of opposition and mockery. This means you Noah are highly successful. I look on you and your family with favor and intend to bless you. Look to me with renewed faith. It is almost time for the rain to start."

Foresight

~

"Look Noah, the animals are coming, and they are restless. They sense the impending doom and are impatient to enter the ark. It is time for you to open the door," declared the Lord.

The animals approached, the ordinary ones two by two, the clean ones seven by seven. They jostled to move forward, pushing their heads against and past the rear of those ahead. Yet each set stayed together as they marched past the cages on their right and left. Each went directly into to the particular cage that Noah had prepared it. Some birds and smaller animals simply came to rest in a common open space.

There are small holes in the port and starboard of the ship below the water line. These are plugged with wooden plugs. The plugs can be pulled so water will channel through various troughs and pipes to the cages for the animals to drink. Most of the holes will remain open after the ark is floating to allow sufficient flow of ocean water (not yet salty) to the many creatures.

The lowest of the three decks have rows of bins on either side of the boat. The bins are filled with wheat, barley, and hay. In the center between the rows of bins is a thirty-foot space running the length of the ark where the dung and urine will collect. The second deck spans across the entire width of the ark. Two-foot wide grates run lengthways along the center of this deck above the dung area below for the dung to fall down through.

There are rows of rectangular openings on the second deck through which the food bins from below protrude up one foot at this time. The animals will feed from these bins. As the food level is eaten down in the bins, Noah's sons will harness the powerful elephants to ropes running through block and tackle to each bin. The elephants will pull the bins upward one foot, one at a time.

Then the sons will move the large iron wood dowels up to the

A New Start

next hole in the vertical posts—which rise alongside each bin—to hold the bins at the new level. Finally, the sons will pull boards off the sides of the bins down to the food level, so the animals can reach more wheat, barley, and hay. When the animals eat the food level down another foot, the process will be repeated. Noah expects the bins to be nearly empty by the time everyone has left the ark.

With this self-feeding setup, the Noah family will not have to try to carry food to all the animals, an impossible task for eight people. The ballast weight from the food, now stored on the first deck, will gradually be replaced with ballast weight from the dung. This will keep the boat stable in the waves of the worldwide flood.

The outside walls of the ark rise from the bottom of the ship to within twenty inches of the roof. Two feet in from these walls—sitting on the highest deck—other walls rise all the way to the roof rafters. There are no floorboards in the two-foot hall space between these walls. This allows the methane gas from below to escape up through the two-foot hall and out the twenty-inch space just below the roof.

The eight Noah-family souls will reside on the upper deck along with any other persons who might decide in this last hour to come on board. Food dispensers feed the smaller animals which are free to roam on part of this deck. These animals will excrete their waste in boxes. Pipes connected to the boxes will channel the waste to the dung space in the bilge.

At least two thousand animals are on the ark. However, only one set of each species (two or seven) is on the ship. Not every variation is here that might have developed from the species.

After the animals were all on board, Noah, his wife, his three sons and their wives entered. Not one other person feared God enough to enter.

Creeeek. Blam. God shut the door of the ark. From the depths of the earth a great phenomenon was about to burst forth,

Foresight

The pre-flood earth probably had only one very large super-continent covered with lush vegetation. There were seas and major rivers. The mountains were smaller than today's, but perhaps 9000 feet high.

The pre-flood earth had a lot of subterranean water; about half of what is now in our oceans. This water was contained in interconnected chambers forming a thin spherical shell about half a mile thick perhaps 10 miles below the earth's surface.

Increasing pressure in the subterranean water stretched the crust, just as the balloon stretches when the pressure inside increases.

Failure in the crust began with a microscopic crack which grew in both directions at about 3 miles per second. The crack, following the path of least resistance, encircled the globe in about two hours.

As the crack raced around the earth, the overlaying rock crust opened up like a rip in a tightly stretched cloth. The subterranean water was under extreme pressure because the weight of the 10 miles of rock pressing down on it.

So the water exploded violently out of the rupture. All along this globe-encircling rupture fountains of water jetted supersonically almost 20 miles into the atmosphere. The spray from this enormous fountain produced torrential rains such as the earth has ever experienced, before or after.

Some of the water, jetting high above the cold stratosphere, froze into super-cooled ice crystals and produced some massive ice dumps; burying, suffocating and instantly freezing many animals, including the frozen mammoths of Siberia and Alaska.

A New Start

The high-pressure fountains eroded the rock on both sides of the crack producing huge volumes of sediments that settled out of this muddy water all over the earth. These sediments trapped and buried plants and animals forming the fossil record.

This erosion widened the rupture. Eventually the width was so great that the compressed rock, beneath the subterranean chamber, sprung upward; giving birth to the mid-oceanic ridge that wraps the earth like the seam of a baseball.

The continental plates, the hydro plates, still with lubricating water beneath them, slid downhill away from the rising mid-Atlantic ridge.

After the massive, slowly accelerating continental plates reached speeds of about 45 miles per hour, they ran into resistance, compressed and buckled. The portions of the hydro plate that bucked down formed ocean trenches. Those that buckled upward formed mountains. This is why the major mountain chains are parallel to the oceanic ridges from which they slid.

The hydro plates, in sliding away from the oceanic ridges, opened up very deep ocean basins into which the flood waters retreated. On the continents each bowl-shaped depression, or basin, was naturally left brim full of water; producing many post-flood lakes.[2]

As the earth convulsed in this way everyone on earth was terrified. Many rushed the ark, pounded on the hull, and plead for Noah to open the door. Several came with a great iron bar to pry the

---

[2] This is a theory proposed by Dr. Walter Brown, The retired director of one the defense department's major research and development laboratories, and the Center for Scientific Creation. The publishers of writings on this theory permit anyone to copy any portion of it.

Foresight

door open. They tried to poke this instrument between the door and the door posts to no avail. Pleading and screaming, more people swarmed the ship only to soon be swept away by the currents. In time the ark began to rise. For forty days and nights it rained. For 150 days the water surged upward above the highest mountain. All flesh outside the ark except the animals of the sea perished.

The currents and wind pushed the ark on a slow, northeasterly voyage with huge rock drift anchors hanging by ropes from the stern into the water below the faster moving current on the surface. This way, the slower moving deep water held the stern back while the faster moving water on the surface forced the bow to point directly down-current. Otherwise the ship would have ridden parallel with the crests of the waves and rocked every creature on board back and forth, unmercifully.[3]

Shem stroked his salt and pepper beard with a glow in his eyes as he gazed upward to the rafters, "What a God we serve. He helped us build a ship that could withstand this great deluge. When we were building the ark, I only had a vague idea of what was to come, but now as I see how well our boat handles the flood, I am overwhelmed with God's goodness, wisdom, and power."

"Yes, my brother," said the darker haired Ham as he pressed his hands against the side planks, "our ship floats. It keeps itself aright and sails through the waves without much rocking and lurching. We have a sound ship due to the mercy of God and our father's Godly understanding of the Lord's directives."

With her large blue-green eyes sparkling, Mrs. Ham straightened her slump on the hay bale, "Well, I agree with both of you, but I am still a bit frightened. And Oh. What is there to go back to when the flood waters drain away, if they ever do?"

---

[3] The shape and proportions of the ark were like many modern merchant ships, showing that the design was what modern ship technology considers to be the best.

A New Start

"Don't you think the God who brought us this far will help us face what is ahead?" inserted Mrs. Noah, leaning her head of golden hair into her slightly wrinkled hands with elbows resting on the sturdy olive wood table where she sat. "We must keep our eyes of faith on the Lord."

"Yes. Yes. You are right Mother. Why should I doubt and be afraid? God will take care of us all the way."

Noah eased himself up, his aged knees creaking, to a standing position as he lifted his hands for attention. Then with voice crackling from hundreds of years of preaching, he boomed, "My dear family, how happy I am that you have been true to your faith and weathered all the mocking and skepticism. I know you endured a lot, but I would be very sad if one of you had stayed behind. That would have been too much to bear."

"Father. Father. How much we all love you and owe our lives to you?" responded Japheth with earnest eyes as he raised his arms and folded his hands over his graying, slightly reddish beard.

"Yes. Yes. We do. We do love you Father," came replies from various members of the family.

After the first 150 days the waters quit rising and the ark came to rest on the mountains of Ararat. Then the waters receded for another 150 days until the tops of the mountains were visible. Forty days later Noah sent out a raven and a dove. The dove returned, not having found any trees to perch on. Obviously the water level, although below the mountain peaks, had not receded to the timberline. The raven did not return. Evidently it found carcasses on which to feed above the timberline. Seven days later Noah sent out the dove again. This time it returned in the evening with a freshly plucked olive leaf in her beak. Seven days later he sent out the dove for the third time and it did not return.

Noah tilted his happy face upward; speaking through lips, parting mustache and beard, he announced, "We have been on the ark a total

Foresight

of 378 days. I believe it might be time to go outside."

Japheth opened his eyes wide, wrinkling his forehead, "Do you really think we should? We have been in here so long I am afraid of the outside world."

"I feel the same way," said Mrs. Noah with dread in her eyes. "The ark has been our haven for so long I dread to face anything outside. Maybe we should just stay here for a while longer."

Mrs. Ham looked at her mother-in-law with a teasing smile. "Mother, have you forgotten what you told me about God taking care of us in the future?"

"Yes. Yes. Yes I have. Open the hatch my husband."

Noah climbed up the ladder and lifted the hatch. "Praise the Lord! Everything is dry," he cried.

~

"Well daughters, wives of my beloved sons, what a sad picture lies before us. Evidently the whole earth is covered with the grayish mud we see before us."

Mrs. Shem looked on with tears streaming down her fair cheeks, "Oh mother. I cannot bear the thoughts that come to my mind. All of what we knew is under that mud, our cattle, our shrubs, our fruit trees, and our neigh... Oh no."

"Well I don't suppose we are at where we lived before the flood. We could be a thousand miles from there, but no doubt things are just as bad where we lived," noted Mrs. Noah.

Mrs. Ham closed her eyes, trying to see what should have been, "If only people would have listened and gone with us into the ark. I tried so hard to convince my best friend, Tamar, to take God seriously. She was always polite but looked on me with pity to think I would believe in God and his declaration of coming judgment."

"Well you know Atheist's idea that the world and all life came into being spontaneously became very popular," said Mrs. Japheth.

A New Start

"People wanted an idea like that to cling to, because they didn't want to believe in God. They didn't want to believe in God because they didn't want to be accountable to a supreme being and his will. They wanted to live as they pleased. No wonder they were gullible enough to swallow atheistic teachings.

Mrs. Japheth stared into the distance, her gorgeous, smooth cheeks reflecting the sunlight, "You know I have a thought. It is probably ridiculous but listen to my idea. I am thinking that the dead creatures and plants buried under this mud will leave formations and eventually turn to rock. After thousands of years, the formations may be discovered some way. Now here comes my wild idea, do you suppose people who don't want to believe in God several thousands of years from now might try to convince themselves that plants, animals, and people evolved from the life forms that made those formations. They might even think those impressions in the rocks were millions of years old instead of just thousands of years old."

"Wow. You really have an imagination, daughter, but I suppose anything is possible. Well my ladies, we have a lot to do to begin life all over again. But where will we start? Where, oh where, will we start?" Mrs. Noah spoke.

"Have you forgotten again, Mother? We must start with faith in God," declared Mrs. Shem with her beautiful smile.

"Yes, of course. Thank you for reminding me again. We must pray and trust God. He will show us the way."

~

Noah sat on a log viewing the devastation all around him this evening: How can I ever find courage at my age of six hundred and one to rebuild? And even if I do, how can I have any confidence that God would not again flood everything with water? The boys seemed to be lukewarm in their love for God, especially Ham. I am not sure they have what it takes to foster a godly society.

Foresight

Suddenly a voice boomed from above, loud and clear, "Noah, my faithful servant. Do not be discouraged. I am not through with you yet. I have a great future planned and I want to give you confidence." God continued:

> "I have set my bow in the cloud, and it shall be a sign of the covenant between me and the earth. When I bring clouds over the earth and the bow is seen in the clouds, I will remember my covenant that is between me and you and every living creature of all flesh. And the waters shall never again become a flood to destroy all flesh. When the bow is in the clouds, I will see it and remember the everlasting covenant between God and every living creature of all flesh that is on the earth." God said to Noah, "This is the sign of the covenant that I have established between me and all flesh that is on the earth" (Genesis 9:13-17).

Not far away each member of the Noah family heard the pronouncement. A soft rain began to mist the atmosphere. And there it was, the most beautiful sight they had ever seen. The bright, glowing bow stretched its red, orange, green, blue indigo, violet, colors all across the western sky.

"How beautiful!" gasped Mrs. Noah and Mrs. Ham in unison.

"What a sight to behold. Yes. Amazing. I'm so overwhelmed," others exclaimed.

"How uplifting," breathed Noah. "I feel those glowing colors ebb into every recess of my being to revitalize my spirit. God is so good."

All heartily agreed, "Yes. Yes. Yes. Yes. Yes."

* * *

Michael turned to Gabriel from where they looked on in the spirit world. Their hearts warmed by the happiness they beheld. "I am really intrigued by the *covenant* of the rainbow. It promises God will never again flood the whole earth with water. This is a *covenant* with all creatures, even the animals, but it does not assign any terms to creation for keeping it. Therefore, the creatures of the earth cannot break the covenant because there are no terms for them to break."

Michael nodded yes, "This is different from the conditional covenant God made with Adam and Eve. I am inclined to believe God will make another covenant with his people which will be conditional as well. God will assign people a part to keep covenant with him as he did with the first couple. As of now, God continues to build his faith-path through his *remnant* of people like Noah. Biblical history will say:

"By faith Noah, being warned by God concerning events as yet unseen, in reverent fear constructed an ark for the saving of his household. By this he condemned the world and became an heir of the righteousness that comes by faith" (Hebrews 11:7).

Abel recognized his need of a blood sacrifice to atone for his sins. Enoch followed course by focusing on pleasing God. Noah was moved by his *faith-driven* godly fear to save his family. These three examples sum up to these three basic facts: God requires a blood sacrifice, he calls people to focus on pleasing him, and he intends for these, his followers to do whatever is required to save their families from the destruction of sin. This is the beginning of the faith-path for the *remnant* to follow.

Foresight

Chapter 4

Secular Humanism Introduced

Gabriel closed his eyes and sighed, "Will humans never learn? Are they hopelessly bent on perverting God's truth and his ways? I cannot believe what the great-grandson of Noah has stooped to.... This guy is using his natural, God-given charisma to lead a revolt against the Lord. He is so taken up with himself, he has lost all fear of the Lord. He hates the Lord simply because he is jealous of the worship people give him. Nimrod wants all of the adoration and worship belonging to God."

Michael shook his head, "Nimrod is filled with *humanism*, the evil system that refuses to acknowledge the need to depend on God. Satan seems to have full control of this narcissist's faculties."

"What is God going to do about this? He has promised to never destroy everything again with a flood."

The angels looked on.

* * *

The wine-drinking, red-faced King Nimrod stood before the

Foresight

large crowd in purple garb with gold and silver lace. His golden crown sparkled with a hundred gleaming gems and glowing pearls. "Ladies and gentlemen of our noble city-state, I am *proud* to announce that we, the secular progressive people of Babel, are ready to erect the greatest edifice ever built in the world. And the really exciting thing is that we have drawn up the plans, set up the administration, and organized the work force without consulting God. We purposely did all of this on our own to demonstrate that we can operate better apart from *faith* in God and his restrictive directions.

"My great-grandfather cooperated with God and built the ark. And how did God repay him for his faithfulness? He sent the great flood to destroy everything he owned and everyone but Noah's family. If Noah had refused to build the ark, God wouldn't have flooded the earth, knowing there would be no survivors to repopulate the earth."

"Now God wants us to have lots of children and scatter across the earth, so we won't become a mighty empire. We know how to deal with God. We will build a tower so high that anyone looking up to see God will see the tower. This will remind them that we are a people great enough to operate apart from God. You don't have to place your faith in the Lord, worship him, and be his victims. If you need a god, let me be your god. I will gladly receive all of your worship, adoration, and praise."

The excited, pumped crowd erupted with the chant they knew so well,

"We worship King Nimrod, protector of Mother Earth.

"We worship King Nimrod, lord of all prideful people.

"We worship King Nimrod to make a name for ourselves."

Nimrod raised his clenched fists in the air and continued, "The tower will always keep us conscious of what God did in Noah's time. By it our children and grandchildren will always be reminded that God is ruthless and unworthy of our worship. I cannot emphasize

Secular Humanism Introduced

enough that we must defy God. For even as I now speak, he is trying to send another flood," Nimrod shouted.

The people gasped.

"What?" many cried in unison.

"Scientists say that an increasing amount of warm air being generated from our rapidly multiplying population could melt the glaciers and bring a flood. That is why God wants us to multiply and spread. He wants us to spread the warming across the earth. God wants to trick us into bringing a flood on ourselves. Will we fall for His scheme?"

"No. No. No!" the people shouted.

"I am happy to see your spunk. Are we really ready to defy God?"

"Yes. Yes. Yes."

"Can we defy God and build the tower?" urged Nimrod.

"Yes, we can.

"Yes, we can.

"Yes, we can.

"Yes, we can.

"Yes, we can.

"Yes, we can," the crowd chanted, drunk with passion.

Sheba, with ashen face and wide brown eyes, turned to Gether where they were standing on the edge of the crowd. "I can't believe how gullible this crowd is! Don't they know the rainbow is a promise that God will never flood the whole earth with water again?"

Gether looked off into the clouded sky with furled brow, "That's the problem. They have lost faith in God's promises because they worship themselves and a person like Nimrod who mirrors their self-centeredness. Losing hope in God also makes them earthly and inclined to worship the universe."

"Yes, and King Nimrod plays their ignorance to the fullest. By convincing the people they face a catastrophe from another flood, he sets them up to gladly accept his solution as well as his control. Then later he can say, 'See. By my leadership, we outsmarted God and averted another flood. I am your savior.'"

"I never thought of that. I believe you are right, Sheba."

"Nimrod will say anything to get people to think he is the greatest. Remember, this is the same guy who claimed he invented the mason trowel until someone discovered that trowels were used before he was born."

Gether shook his head in disgust, "Yah, but the people like Nimrod because they identify with his self-centered, humanistic pride. You heard their chant. They are determined to make a name for themselves by showing that they can effectively operate in their own strength and understanding apart from *faith* in God. I've never seen such like-minded, though misguided, purpose!"

"Do you think their unity is true unity?" mused Sheba.

"Humm. Good question."

~

The building had begun. Lud shouted through drawn, taut lips, "Elishah, get that pile of bricks over here. Can't you see that I have a whole batch of mortar mixed up and need to use it up before dark?"

"Who made you boss, you son of Ham? I have enough to do to keep others supplied."

"Are you looking for a fight, son of Japheth?"

On the other side of the tower, Mash and Hador were getting along no better.

Big-eared Hador leaned forward and glared at Mash, "How is it that we Semites do more work on this tower than anyone else, but we never get promoted to leadership positions?"

"What did you expect? You should have known that the Hamites would get all of the good positions when you convinced me to work here. Did you forget that King Nimrod is a son of Ham? The money

Secular Humanism Introduced

you were offered to recruit me made you blind to the Hamites intentions to take advantage of us."

"Yes, Hador, just look at me through those blue, accusing eyes past your big nose and blame it all on me. Don't you think I feel bad enough?"

"No, you don't. I hope the Hamites work you very hard."

In the construction office, another heated conversation occurred between Peleg and the personnel director, Dodan.

"Why did you Semite chaps initiate that fight with the sons of Japheth?" asked Dodan, with drawn face as he leaned forward with his hands propped on his waist and elbows pointed out.

"It was to teach you Japhethites a lesson for siding with the Hamites in their plot to keep all of us Semites from supervisory positions," replied Peleg.

"Nonsense. You sons of Shem just don't have leadership qualities," responded Dodan with a smug smile.

"How dare you? Everyone knows that our people accomplish more than anyone else because they are efficient. You lazy Japhethites would really be hurting to make a showing if it were not for us. No wonder you don't want us to leave the hands-on work."

"Those are fighting words, Peleg."

Meanwhile, at the top of the twenty-foot tower structure, King Nimrod demanded an explanation from the building superintendent, "Naph, you are way behind schedule. This tower was supposed to be thirty feet high by now. What do you have to say for yourself?"

"O King. Have mercy on your faithful servant. The problem is with the sons of Shem. They slack in their work."

"No we don't!" cried Peleg from behind Nimrod, "and we're not going to be the scapegoats any longer!"

But all Nimrod heard from Peleg was the babble of scrambled syllables. Turning, he shouted to the captain of his guard, "Cas, take him away and cut off his head for spewing such disrespectful prattle

Foresight

in my ears." This time it was Cas who heard nothing but babble. Trembling, he stood there, wide-eyed and uncomprehending.

Red-faced Nimrod swirled back to face Naph with piercing eyes. "What is going on…?" But he swirled too fast, lost his balance, and fell headfirst to the ground. His stiffened frame drove his face into the dirt. Then his body flipped to the side and landed perpendicular to the wall. Blood spurted out of his head, soaking into the dry earth.

Silence prevailed for a moment. Then suddenly, everyone began shouting commands and curses, but their words were only babble. Eyes stared and widened. Faces turned from one to the other. Voices stuttered and stammered. Countenances showed confusion and shame. *Prideful* self-confidence shattered and symbolically followed Nimrod's deadly plunge to the ground. Silently the workers lowered themselves to the earth and gravitated to Nimrod's body in a daze.

Mechanically they lifted him and carried him away. Hours later he regained consciousness just long enough to mutter more incoherent prattle before he expired.

Was he still trying to say, "We can operate better apart from *faith* in God?"

Chapter 5

Systematic Idolatry Invented

"You hideous, fallen imps of the abyss, you abominable devils who go to and fro across the earth, I have called you to this meeting to answer for your mismanagement of Babel. I, Satan, the brilliant strategist of all evil and falsehood, had the greatest thing going since I successfully plotted Adam and Eve's downfall in the Garden of Eden.

"My glory was evident in the passion to build the tower. The hearts of all the self-centered people were aligned to defy God. I had everyone deceived into thinking he did his own thing even as he followed my bidding. The first full-blown development of *secular humanism* was in place. Each person proudly trusted himself and the collective human effort. It was really uplifting to see how I got the people to purposely rule God out of their plans. Those gullible humans ate out of my hand. They lived just to pleasure their senses instead of finding the joy of the Lord through prayer and fellowship with God.

"Then, when I turned things over to you inferior devils, people started fighting and falling into discord. And horror of horrors, it became evident that the unity I had formed was not based on a true concern for the community as I had led everyone to believe. When each one started speaking his own language, the truth was out: everyone was into the project for what he could get out of it for himself. Each one was speaking his own language in his heart until his self-centeredness finally gave vent to speaking his own language audibly. Then no one understood his fellows or was understood by them.

"What a shameful exposure of our inability to bring true harmony to a community. That situation left us wide open for future generations to hammer us with the truth that the only true unity is to be found in God's *love*. Yuck. What a distasteful reality. Now speak up, professors of falsehood, how is it that you blundered so badly?"

"Satan, you obnoxious egotist," cried Aga. "How dare you blame the failure at Babylon on us? You were so full of your ugly self, that you overreached reality. As you have just acknowledged, the unity you formed was not a true concern for the community and therefore not a true unity. You should have known that such a unity would not last."

"Aga, you insubordinate blow gun, I should put you in confinement."

"But I have something important to contribute," protested Aga.

"It had better be something really good, or off you go to solitary confinement. I have had enough of you."

"Well before we plan anything, we must remind ourselves that we cannot do anything noble like uniting a community to accomplish something worthwhile. All we can do is pervert and corrupt. Therefore, our plans must be limited to perversion and corruption."

"Aga, you scoundrel. This is why I hate you so much. You always persist in reminding us of ugly truths. The only truth I want to hear about is the one that shows how to effectively destroy God's purposes," Satan spouted.

"But you see, Detestable One, we must face this unlikable truth to know where we made our mistake and how to proceed from here on. When we try to do something noble, we fail. We need to return to our pre-flood policies that brought about the destruction of all the inhabitants of the earth but the Noah family. We need to saturate people's hearts with *materialistic* greed and *sensualistic* pleasure. Sensualism makes them obsessed with gratifying their senses. They become lovers of pleasure rather than lovers of God.[4] *Materialism* makes them place their main *hope* in earthly things rather than in God and spiritual things.[5] We need to get them to totally sell out to these drives.

"We learned in the Garden of Eden that the very nature of *sensualism* and *materialism* turns people from *loving* God and placing *hope* in Him. These avenues to sin cause people to live only for pleasuring their senses instead of living in the joy of the Lord through prayer and fellowship with their Maker. Then this naturally leads to the *humanism* of people trusting in themselves. And the more people trust in themselves, the more they idolize material things and sensory pleasure. The cycle keeps going, and fulfillment always seems to be just around the next corner but never realized. So eventually they become disillusioned and filled with *despair*.

"By the way, I have been a good spy. I overheard the angels putting their descriptions on our three -isms. They call sensualism 'the lust of the flesh.' Materialism they call the 'lust of the eyes.' And they call humanism 'the pride of life.'"[6]

"Oh really," snarled Satan. "Well back to our planning, I have a concern that we do this in the right way. I fear mankind will develop technologies out of *materialistic* greed which could be used to

---

[4] See 2 Timothy 3:4
[5] See Matthew 6:19
[6] I John 2:16

advance God's kingdom. For example, they could use the high-quality bricks they developed for building the Babylon tower to build structures for promoting God's cause. I also fear the obsession with sensory pleasure could drive people to do some good. Even though the passion is purely selfish, it could end up doing nice things for others and coming dangerously close to promoting real love."

"Well we cannot expect everything to go our way, but we can count on this strategy to bring many to *despair*."

"But Aga, when people come to utter *despair*, they may recognize that they need God. Then they will turn to God and forever be beyond our reach."

"That could be, but we may have to take that risk. Don't forget when they come to the end of themselves, we can offer other alternatives…."

"Like suicide?" asked Satan with an evil grin.

"Yes, like suicide—or a death wish that will make them abandon themselves to moral recklessness," replied Aga.

"We can be sure that *self-centeredness* leads to *despair* all right," said Satan.

"You speak from experience, don't you, Detestable One," taunted Aga. "You and all of us miserable imps have experienced multi-millenniums banished from God's presence because of your self-centered scam to get us to worship you. For this, God relegated us to your domain in which we have no capacity for true *love* or any meaningful *faith* and *hope*. Oh, how dumb of us to think we could advance ourselves by worshiping you."

"You foulmouthed, ugly, stinking devil. How dare you!" screamed Satan. "Duba and Ducuss. Take Aga away and put him in solitary confinement until he learns some respect."

Duba and Ducuss ran and pounced upon Aga and carried him away as his angry curses gradually faded in the distance.

"Now listen up, you devils," shouted Satan. "Aga is hopelessly

Systematic Idolatry Invented

bitter at me because he has turned away from hating God. In doing so he has given up the only hope we have—the hope of getting back at God. Hating God gives us energy to destroy God's purposes. So by nurturing hatred for God, we will eventually prevail and have our revenge.

"As much as I don't like to do so, I have to acknowledge that most of what Aga said is true. We must inspire people to sell out to the *hope* of gaining material goods and the *love* of sensory pleasure. Then we will watch in glee as their passions for these things drive them into greater and greater *despair* and further from God."

"But Lord Satan, how will we inspire people to sell out in this way?" asked An.

"I am open for suggestions," replied Satan. "I see you stand to speak, Enlil. What are your thoughts?"

"My Lord, since people's hearts have a natural longing for God, we must convince them that they are worshiping God by unreservedly giving way to greed and feel-good, sensual desire. Then we need to provide gods that reward them for this kind of worship. Of course, these gods will also punish them when they don't receive the people's worship. The carrot and stick approach will give us control over them."

"What a brilliant idea," cried Satan. "Since the fall in the Garden, people tend to direct the full force of their love to what gratifies their sensory desires. They will be glad to offer acts that gratify these cravings for worship. And as they offer, they will play into the control of the gods who receive their worship. Yet they will think they are exercising freedom to do their own thing. By the time they realize that the gods control them, they will be afraid to turn away for fear of the god's punishment. Ah yes. That will alleviate my concern that *despair* will drive people into God's arms.

"But don't take too much credit for your idea, Enlil. You can never outsmart me. I have been considering the idea of appointing

Foresight

you demons to be gods for a long time. So now that you have reminded me of this, I am ready to appoint you and your fellow demons as gods to control every aspect of people's lives. In doing this we will evolve a new Sumerian culture.[7] This culture could influence humans for hundreds of years to come.

"An, you will be sovereign over the entire physical universe and preside over a council of gods. You will simulate people's elemental sense of need into greed for more and more things. You will do this by constantly parading glamorous material things before their eyes. Then as they develop this greediness of heart you will offer them many things. This will convince them that they can fulfill the deep desires of their hearts by worshiping things.

"Enlil, you will be An's son and command people to worship. An, you will be the lord of the atmosphere who permits people, animals, and plants to breathe, grow and live. You will be a god of justice with power to punish and reward.

"Inanna, you will be the great goddess of Ur—a goddess of love and fertility. I intend for you to become very great. You will stimulate people's elemental sexual drives until they become preoccupied with the quest for sexual pleasure. You will portray lewd displays before their eyes and voice lewd expressions to their ears. This will cause them to lust for the illicit sex our gods offer.

"Dumuzi, you will be Inanna's husband and help advance her sexual exploits.

"Nanna you will be a close associate of Inanna. You will be the god of the moon and stimulate people's elemental need for prestige to have *pride* in their own understanding. These thoughts will cause them to lean to their own understanding, not knowing that this understanding comes from the thoughts you have injected. You have many talents, so if you do well, I will assign you more

---

[7] The idol worshiping Ur of the Chaldees was in Sumer and a part of Sumerian culture.

Systematic Idolatry Invented

responsibilities.

"Enki, you will be the god of water to make people believe that spiritual beings abide in the water.

Negal, you will be the god of war to make people believe warring is a godly activity.

"Ninnsun, I pronounce you the goddess of cows to get people to venerate cows.

"Shamash, you will be the sun god to get people to venerate the sun."

On and on, Satan continued to call out the names of his most trusted imps and pronounce each one a god of a domain, element or force. Then a great celebration took place. All the imps danced in glee to their hopes of overcoming God and their ever-pervading *despair*. But their glee did not unite them in love for one another. They had lost all capacity for love. Only their common hatred for God and people bound them in a ruthless united cause to drive people to *despair*.

"Before we go, I have something I need to say," said An. "I also have been a good spy. Well, you know what I mean. I understand "good" is not a politically-correct word."

"Yes, by all means don't be like Aga."

An continued, "Let's say I have been an effective spy. I bugged a disturbing bit of intel from the angels. It is being reported that God has a top-secret, classified plan to deliver mankind from the curse of sin. It is something more than animal sacrifices. We can be sure it has something to do with breaking the power we gained over people through Adam's fall. But beyond that I doubt we will ever know. The angels aren't even privy to the details of this classified intel."

"Oh great!" yelled Satan. "God has no intentions of playing fair. He already has us at a serious disadvantage by limiting how much we can attack people. And now he is developing a secret strategy, so we cannot know how to plan a counterstrategy. This just means we have

Foresight

to redouble our efforts to drive people to *despair.* Hopefully, those in deep *despair* will not look to any of God's remedies with *hope* in him. Now get out and get to work! All of you, my highly esteemed devils."

Chapter 6

Called Out

The Sumerian New Year celebration was in full swing in Ur. The king of Sumer ceremonially married a priestess of Inanna, the daughter of the moon-god Nanna, to recreate the marriage of Inanna to Dumuzi. It was imagined that their sexual union would give fertility to the land and power to the king. The sacred prostitutes gave themselves to the male worshipers as an expression of Inanna's rapacious appetite for men. And men representing Dumuzi offered their services to the female worshipers.

Another priestess of Inanna danced in the center of the crowd. One by one she stripped off her many jewels and then her articles of clothing until she was entirely naked. Finally, she fell to the ground into a coma-like state. Rapid-pace dancing shook the earth. The screaming cries to the gods pierced the night air. Men and women alike fell to the ground, drunk with strong wine.

Late the next morning, Nahor awoke to a splitting headache. Cursing, he struggled to rise from his bed. His brother Haran lay red-faced nearby, as still as death. The other brother, Abram, was walking

Foresight

the floor. He had not engaged in the revelries, but his conscience smote him for having attended the evil celebration.

He felt drained of all spiritual energy and God seemed far away. If only God would speak to him, he would never again go to the festivities of the gods. He would never again be a bad influence on others by allowing himself to be seen at such a place. If only he had taken his stand, his younger brothers might not have gone to the celebration. He cringed at the memory of Haran in the shadows. Hopefully, Haran's son Lot had not been nearby to see his father with the prostitute.

"Father, how could we have come to such disgrace?" Abram said to Terah, who sat bleary-eyed in the corner of the room.

"Aw, son. Don't bother me with your moralizing. Everybody has to have an outlet for the dark cravings of his soul now and then. Furthermore, we should play our part in bringing the land to fertility," Terah answered.

"Father, have you too been deceived by that lie? Sexual immorality only serves to contaminate our souls as well as our bodies and to bring the wrath of God upon us."

"Son. Be off with you. I am too sick to listen to your chatter."

Shocked into silence, Abram turned to gaze at his wife, Sarai. She rushed over, wrapped her arms around him, and sobbed against his chest. After a time, he gently pushed her away and wandered outside. He drifted down the path toward the sheepfold.

"Oh Lord," Abram cried, "we are in the grips of Satan's snare. Our situation is hopeless. My relatives have lost their faith. We are sold out to the worship of the gods. Our self-centeredness is driving us to madness. We live just to pleasure our senses instead of living in the joy of the Lord through pray and fellowship with God. I have sinned along with the rest of my family. Oh Lord, have mercy on us and deliver us from this place."

Abram slumped down on the rock outside the sheepfold and sat staring into the northwest for a long time. Gradually he resolved to do something drastic to save his family's future.

"Abram. Abram. Abram!" cried Terah as he ran down the path toward Abram.

"What is the matter, Father?" Abram responded, quickly rising to his feet.

"Oh my son. My son. Your brother Haran is dead."

~

Standing beside the gravesite with Abram, Terah said, "Abram, your brother's death has brought me to my senses. We need to get as far from Ur as possible. The sad thing is that we are leaving our ancestral fathers. But they are not making any moves to separate themselves from the abominable idolatry.

"God wants us out of here, but you know the Lord far better than I. You are sensitive to his leadership, so you lead the way. If only I had a relationship with God like you have. Because of my wickedness, Haran is dead and Nahor's heart is sold out to the culture of Ur. Oh how my heart breaks to leave them. But we must get away."

"Father, you must not take all the blame. You only destroy valuable energy beating up yourself over the past. From now on, we must urgently press toward the goal of finding God's plan for our future and living out that faith-path. I agree that we must leave this place. How I will miss our relatives! Yet moving on will help us find God's will for our lives. The lay of the land northwest along the Euphrates River provides a good route. We will take that route and I believe that the farther we get from Ur, the more I will see and know God."

~

In spite of the Abram family's inconsolable grief over the death of Haran, their days of mourning had been cut short. Even the refusal

Foresight

of Nahor to join them had not deterred them. Terah, Abram, Sarai, and Abram's nephew Lot pressed ahead on their caravan of camels. Many days later, they woke from their night's sleep along the path. The morning sun was just over the horizon. Abram said, "Sarai, the further we go, the greater peace I have."

"Not just you, my husband. My body hurts from riding that camel and the eerie sounds of the night keep me awake. But I feel a great reassuring peace."

"Thank you for telling me that, Sarai; I pray that Father and Lot will come to know the Lord as we do. I worry about them. If they don't have a real encounter with the Lord, they could soon be back to idol worship. And oh how I weep over Nahor. How could he be so deceived as to think he has a future in Ur?"

From outside came a voice, "Weep no more, my brother." Abram leaped through the flap-opening of the tent and exclaimed, "Nahor. Nahor. I cannot believe my eyes. You have come!" The brothers embraced and wept on each other's shoulders.

"Where is Milcah, your wife?" cried Sarai.

"She is down by the river bathing, as I was. It had been three days since we bathed, because we were so eager to catch up with you. She will be here shortly," Nahor explained.

Terah and Lot sprang from their tent. "My son, you have come. You have come. How glad I am to see you," cried Terah, rushing to embrace Nahor.

"Seeing your face, my Father, gives me more warmth than this morning sun. And Lot, it is good to find you looking so vigorous. You look so much like your father. If only Haran could be here with us," Nahor said, lowering his face in grief.

"I miss him greatly, my uncle, but his memory reminds me to press forward to the life he should have had."

Soon Milcah arrived and joined the happy reunion. Then with light hearts and jubilant spirits, the company pressed on with their journey. For many months of strong, dusty winds and hot sun, they continued their travel in a northwesterly direction along the Euphrates. Finally, they arrived at the fork of the Balikh River and turned north to follow it. Many days later they came to a plain in northern Mesopotamia. They named it Haran and settled to reside there. Here for years they built large flocks of sheep and herds of goats.

~

Nahor and Milcah had children. As they grew, their children acquired friends. Their friends invited them to the worship of the Moon god, Sin, another name for the demon Nanna.

"No children, you cannot go," declared Nahor.

"Father, why do you cling to your old-fashioned beliefs? Are you afraid of what Abram will say?" Bethuel, Nahor's son asked.

"As I have told you many times, children, your mother and I learned in Ur that idol worship leads to all kinds of evil. I want no part of this Sin worship."

"Aw, Father," said Bethuel. "My friends say that Sin worship is not anything like the Inanna worship in Sumer. In fact, none of my friends actually worship Sin. They just go to the Sin celebrations to join in the festivities. Everybody goes to the festivities. If we don't go people will think we are weird, and they will look on you as a troublemaker. This society really doesn't like people who think they are too good to go to the festivities."

Milcah chimed in, "My husband, we need to be open minded. If Sin worship is just a form and not true worship, then our children would not be rejecting the Lord if they merely go to the festivities." On and on, Milcah and the children clamored, pled, and cajoled.

"All right, my children, I will let you go, but I don't want you to do anything that actually constitutes the worship of the moon god, Sin," said Nahor.

Foresight

~

"Oh Lord, not again. Not again. My brother's family is being lured back into idol worship. They keep telling me that they are only participating in certain cultural activities and not really worshiping the moon god, but they are deceived. They dance with the rest at the lewd Sin celebrations and corrupt their moral instincts. How could they so blindly do Sin's bidding and then believe they are exercising freedom to do as they choose? If only my father, Terah, had not died, he could help me restrain them," Abram cried out to God.

"Abram, if you stay in Haran your offspring will be lured to worship idols like the rest of Haran."

"Lord, is that you who spoke, or am I losing my mental faculties through the tremendous stress I am under?"

> Now the Lord said to Abram, "Go from your country and your kindred and your father's house to the land that I will show you. And I will make of you a great nation, and I will bless you and make your name great, so that you will be a blessing. I will bless those who bless you, and him who dishonors you I will curse, and in you all the families of the earth shall be blessed" (Genesis 12:1-3).

Abram answered, "Lord, I have heard you. I embrace the relationship with you as you've just offered it to me. Tomorrow we will start out for the Promised Land."

~

Abram sat in his tent with his head cupped in his hands staring out into the night. "Lord, you have blessed me in this Promised Land, but I am having some doubts," said Abram. "How can you give me the future you have promised through my descendants when I don't have even one child?" God took him outside and said:

> "Look toward heaven, and number the stars, if you are able to number them." Then he said to him, "So shall your offspring

be." And he believed the Lord, and he counted it to him as righteousness (Genesis 15:5-6).

On that day the Lord made a covenant with Abram, saying, "To your offspring I give this land, from the river of Egypt to the great river, the river Euphrates, the land of the Kenites, the Kenizzites, the Kadmonites, the Hittites, the Perizzites, the Rephaim, the Amorites, the Canaanites, the Girgashites and the Jebusites" (Genesis 15:18-21).

* * *

Gabriel's eyes brightened as he contemplated, This confirmation of the covenant God made with Abram when he called him out of Haran is very interesting. Then God promised to make Abram into a great, blessed nation and to bless all the peoples of the earth through him. Now in this confirmation God has promised him a huge number of descendants to receive the blessing and he specified the exact location for where this blessing will be received. The Lord has even specified the boundaries of the Promised Land.

Michael hovered over Gabriel with a broad smile at seeing the messenger angel in deep thought. "Are you contemplating what the full meaning of the covenant is? Could you be thinking about what all the blessing to the people of the earth entails?"

"You know I am," replied Gabriel.

"Well, I can tell you this much," said Michael. This *covenant* surely has something to do with striking the serpent's head and providing a sufficient atonement for people's sin. It is not just about God blessing people materially.

"Let's review the faith-path God has built for the purpose of having a blessed nation to bless the other nations of the earth: Abel recognized his need of a blood sacrifice to atone for his sins. Enoch followed course and focused on pleasing God. Noah was moved by his faith-driven godly fear to save his family. Abram was called out from idolatry to go to a land God would show him. Biblical history

Foresight

will show the faith of these four patriarchs in verbiage long to be remembered:

> " By faith Abel offered to God a more acceptable sacrifice than Cain, through which he was commended as righteous, God commending him by accepting his gifts. And through his faith, though he died, he still speaks.
>
> "By faith Enoch was taken up so that he should not see death, and he was not found, because God had taken him. Now before he was taken he was commended as having pleased God. And without faith it is impossible to please him, for whoever would draw near to God must believe that he exists and that he rewards those who seek him.
>
> "By faith Noah, being warned by God concerning events as yet unseen, in reverent fear constructed an ark for the saving of his household. By this he condemned the world and became an heir of the righteousness that comes by faith.
>
> By faith Abraham obeyed when he was called to go out to a place that he was to receive as an inheritance. And he went out, not knowing where he was going.
>
> "By faith he went to live in the land of promise, as in a foreign land, living in tents with Isaac and Jacob, heirs with him of the same promise. For he was looking forward to the city that has foundations, whose designer and builder is God" (Hebrews 11:4-10).

These four examples sum up these four basic facts," Michael continued:

1. God requires people to place faith in a blood sacrifice as Abel's actions show.
2. God calls people to focus on pleasing him as Enoch did.
3. God calls his followers to focus on saving their families from the destruction of sin as did Noah.
4. The Lord calls his people to come out from idolatry and follow

his leadership, even if they don't know where it will lead them, as Abraham's life shows.

"Yes. This is the faith-path being developed by God for the *remnant* to follow in keeping his *covenant*."

Foresight

Chapter 7

The Test

Abram was ninety-nine years old. He looked up to heaven, his face aglow with many warm memories of his walk with the Lord, "Many times I have been anxious about how you would bless the world through me as you have promised, my Lord. But I have finally learned to just trust you fully and let you work out the details." Suddenly Abram felt an awesome sense of God's presence and then a voice said:

"I am God Almighty; walk before me, and be blameless, that I may make my covenant between me and you, and may multiply you greatly."

Then Abram fell on his face. And God said to him, "Behold, my covenant is with you, and you shall be the father of a multitude of nations. No longer shall your name be called Abram, but your name shall be Abraham, for I have made you the father of a multitude of nations. I will make you exceedingly fruitful, and I will make you into nations, and kings shall come from you. And I will establish my covenant between me and you and your offspring after you

Foresight

> throughout their generations for an everlasting covenant, to be God to you and to your offspring after you" (Genesis 17:1-7).

* * *

Gabriel's eyebrows lifted, wrinkling his forehead. His eyes glistened alertly. "You know, Michael, God first initiated his *covenant* with Abraham when he called him out of Sumer. Then the Lord promised to bless him and make him a great nation. And through the years God has periodically confirmed the *covenant* with added specific blessings.

"Abram is now ninety-nine years old. And God has again confirmed the covenant with the change of his name to Abraham, meaning the father of multitudes. But this time he instructed Abraham to live in his presence and be blameless before he confirmed it. This implies that Abraham has a part to play in keeping the covenant. Abraham is to be blameless and maintain a relationship with God."

"Yes Gabriel, and this expression of the *covenant* includes the promise that God will confirm the *covenant* with the patriarch's offspring throughout their generations. God must be reserving a *remnant* who will keep his covenant by obeying him throughout history.

"This covenant is different than the covenant God confirmed with the rainbow. The rainbow covenant was with all creatures and it was unconditional. But I doubt this one is unconditional.[8] The Lord can only be the God of the offspring who will keep their part of the covenant by obeying him. Therefore, the Lord must know there will always be a *remnant* who will keep their part to be able say the covenant is permanent."

"I have a feeling we will hear more later to clarify the issue,"

---

[8] See Joshua 24:20

The Test

replied Gabriel.

* * *

Still-beautiful, ninety-year old Sarah laughed inside the tent. "How funny. These men who are outside telling Abraham I am going to have a child don't know about women. After I am worn out and my husband is old, will I have a child? But I want to believe God is speaking. My heart responds to this. Could I have a child even if I am ninety years old? Ha. Ha. Ha. This is really funny, but oh how thrilling it would be to hold my very own baby in my arms!"

~

With the sun shining on Isaac's smooth face and dark hair, he strode up the mountain in the land of Moriah. His father Abraham pressed along beside him. The young man showed the beginnings of a beard on his young chin in contrast to his father's long-flowing beard. The bundle of wood pressed into Isaac's back, the sharp edges causing a bit of discomfort. But he didn't mind because this was to be a special day with his beloved, gray-haired father. They were going to the mountain peak to worship the Lord together.

Abraham's face furrowed with deep, pained lines as he periodically stole glances at the tall, handsome boy. The aged man was thinking, I had to wait until I was a hundred years old for this son to be born. And he is so awesome. He shows no signs of weariness though he has been carrying the wood for three hours. "Oh how I love this fine specimen of humanity!" Abraham said to himself with immense pride.

All the decades of yearning for his wife Sarah to bear a child had built up like water pressure behind a dam. When Isaac arrived out of Sarah's wrinkled body, the dam broke and the love gushed forth to envelope the new baby boy. Abraham thought, "I would do anything for this boy except— well, I love God also. Do the two loves have to be in

Foresight
conflict?"

Abraham trusted the Lord so much he always proceeded to obey God's instructions without delay, no questions asked. This is why he rose early the next morning after God had given him new orders to carry out the task. By this time, Father and son had trekked for three days with the donkey carrying the wood. When they came to the base of the mountain, they left the donkey with the servants and proceeded up the incline.

In spite of Abraham's readiness to obey, he had serious doubts. Did not God promise to bless the world through Isaac and his descendants? Why would God require such an unthinkable deed? He faltered and almost fell over and over again as tremors shot through his whole body.

Isaac was ahead a few steps and didn't notice Abraham, but he was troubled. Why is Father so quiet today? He seems greatly distracted. Is this climb too much for him? I should slow my pace so as not to exhaust my aging father whom I love with all my heart. Abraham noticed his son slowing down and quickly made great effort to compose himself and brace against the tremors as he caught up with the boy.

Suddenly, Isaac frowned with questioning eyes as he looked back and forth from the ground to the burning torch his father held.

> And Isaac said to his father Abraham, "My father!"
> And he said, "Here I am, my son."
> He said, "Behold, the fire and the wood, but where is the lamb for a burnt offering?"
> Abraham said, "God will provide for himself the lamb for a burnt offering, my son"(Genesis 22:7-8).

* * *

"There has to be more to this than just testing father and son," said an angel.

The Test

"I overheard Michael telling someone that God is giving us a picture of some future event," said another. "Has something to do with a top secret, classified operation God is planning." Breathlessly the hosts of angels looked on. Never, since the temptation in the garden, was heaven and hell so pitted against each other.

* * *

The demons also were alert to the situation.

"Now is our opportune time," pronounced the devil. "We need to exert extreme pressure on Isaac. He is strong enough to resist his father. It should be easy to convince him to stay his father's hand. It is time to fan any rebellion he may harbor. When he discovers what Abraham is up to, we can convince him to declare the man incompetent. Then we will get him to enforce his right to take over the family affairs by telling everybody what his father meant to do. God's plan to bless the world through this family will be defeated for lack of direction from the patriarch. We need to get into Isaac's head." With broad-faced grins, the demons high-fived all around with dark anticipation.

Yes. All demons were watching with desperate intensity from the bleachers of the lower heaven along with every one of the angels from the bleachers of the higher heaven. The angels were rooting for Abraham to obey. The demons were cheering for disobedience.

Gabriel stood at rapt attention, ready to cry into the earth's sound waves at the precise instant needed. Would Abraham and Isaac stand the test? What would happen to God's promise if they didn't?

* * *

Comprehension began to dawn on Isaac, *Surely not. God's people never do such things. God never operates out of jealousy or capriciousness.*

Foresight

He always operates out of love. But then Isaac's gaze met his father's penetrating, questioning stare, Oh no. No. I won't submit. Never. Never. It is time to declare my independence. What kind of a God would require my loving father to do such a thing?

Angry tears began flowing down his cheeks, only to be met with huge sobs from Abraham. Father reached out and embraced his son. Isaac wanted to resist, to push the patriarch to the ground, but he felt the warmth of Abraham's spirit. There had always been this amazing spiritual communication between them. They knew they were destined as coworkers to advance the cause of righteousness across the land so marred with ungodliness. The good times they had experienced together flooded their minds. They clung to each other and wept loud and long until they could weep no more.

The heavenly Father looked on, knowing it would be this way with himself and his Son, when they would come to such a moment. What powerful forces of love would be at play, at once in conflict and yet in harmony. The love each had for the other would be in conflict. Their love calling for action *against* each other would at the same time be calling for action *for* each other in their common cause of facilitating higher purposes. What conflict!

* * *

The demons were going crazy. Satan was desperate and in a rage. "Someone help," he cried. "What can we do to overcome this love? We have no resources to conquer Godly love. Are there any wild animals nearby that we could provoke to make an attack?"

"No, most noble, hate-filled Master," cried An. "And besides, the Lord has angels flooding the atmosphere. We don't have a chance."

"Oh terrible. Why didn't you demons, whom I depend on for advice, alert me to a better strategy? I should bust your heads wide open," Satan shouted.

The Test

"Wait," yelled Aga who had just recently been let out of solitary confinement for his insubordination. "Satan, I thought by now you would know our resources are quite limited. We can only hope to operate through hate, despair, and such-like. But these tools can be very effective. Distract Isaac. His emotions are rolling in great conflict. We saw his initial reaction of anger. This emotion is still there. Explode his mind with thoughts of self-love and self-pity. Show him Abraham is thoughtless and unmerciful."

"Have at it, Aga. You have reason to try to redeem yourself from your former criminal actions."

* * *

Sure enough. The thoughts from Aga exploded in Isaac's mind: *Well yes, Father loves me,* Isaac thought, *but this is crazy. Why should I go along with this?*

"My Father, if it is possible, let this cup pass from me,"[9] Isaac said.

Abraham looked straight into Isaac's eyes with amazing compassion written in his eyes and every crease in his face, but he was silent.

"Yet not as I will, but as you will,"[10] added Isaac.

The angels cheered. Satan and his demons slunk off the scene in shame and disgrace.

Father built the altar as the son looked on. Isaac lay bound on it. Abraham raised the knife:

> But the angel of the Lord called to him from heaven and said, "Abraham, Abraham!"
>
> And he said, "Here I am."

---

[9] Matthew 26:39
[10] Matthew 26:39

Foresight

> He said, "Do not lay your hand on the boy or do anything to him, for now I know that you fear God, seeing you have not withheld your son, your only son, from me."
>
> And Abraham lifted up his eyes and looked, and behold, behind him was a ram, caught in a thicket by his horns. And Abraham went and took the ram and offered it up as a burnt offering instead of his son. So Abraham called the name of that place, "The Lord will provide"; as it is said to this day, "On the mount of the Lord it shall be provided."
>
> And the angel of the Lord called to Abraham a second time from heaven and said, "By myself I have sworn, declares the Lord, because you have done this and have not withheld your son, your only son, I will surely bless you, and I will surely multiply your offspring as the stars of heaven and as the sand that is on the seashore. And your offspring shall possess the gate of his enemies, and in your offspring shall all the nations of the earth be blessed, because you have obeyed my voice" (Genesis 22:11-18).

* * *

"God has just renewed the *covenant* relative to Abraham being willing to offer Isaac," said Michael to Gabriel. "The great trauma we just witnessed of Abraham and Isaac resisting all natural instincts to not do what God required, has to be very significant to the future of the *covenant*. Otherwise the Lord would not have renewed the *covenant* in connection with this drama.

"And I have amazing news. The Lord has given you and me access to a source of intel called, 'The Book of Truth.'[11] It contains important information of God's agenda for his kingdom and specific details on what we have just witnessed."

---

[11] See Daniel 10:21

The Test

"Awesome. How do I access the Book of Truth?"

"Tune your spirit to the micro-waves of the spirit world. You will realize the Book of Truth. Enter this key into the book: *the kingdom of God conquers the kingdom of this world.*"

Following these instructions, Gabriel realized his spirit connecting to the Book of Truth. He saw a heading entitled "The Significance of Abraham's Offering in Relation to the *Covenant.*" Below it the text read, "Abraham's and Isaac's father-son experience points to a sin offering which will fulfill the promise implied in all animal sacrifices. This ultimate sin-offering sacrifice will redeem all token sacrifices of animals and deliver from Sheol those who made them. Also, all who believe in the one making the ultimate sacrifice after he makes it will have their sins fully atoned for."

"If only we could know the full mystery!" exclaimed Gabriel.

Michael replied, "We will have to be patient. More intel will be forthcoming. And we must not breathe the details of this, lest Satan catch on. We can only communicate as we are now, through our spirits. God's top-secret, classified intel must not be compromised. Biblical history will record these additional faith acts of Abraham as well as the faith of Sarah:

> " By faith Sarah herself received power to conceive, even when she was past the age, since she considered him faithful who had promised" (Hebrews 11:11).
>
> "By faith Abraham, when he was tested, offered up Isaac, and he who had received the promises was in the act of offering up his only son, of whom it was said, 'Through Isaac shall your offspring be named.' He considered that God was able even to raise him from the dead, from which, figuratively speaking, he did receive him back" (Hebrews 11:17-19).

"Well, I think it is time to review the faith-path for God's *remnant* to follow in keeping his *covenant.* We will review this with Sarah, and add other observations of Abraham," continued Michael.

Foresight
1. God requires people to place faith in a blood sacrifice as Abel's actions show.
2. God calls people to focus on pleasing him as Enoch did.
3. God calls his followers to focus on saving their families from the destruction of sin as did Noah.
4. The Lord calls his people to come out from idolatry and follow his leadership, even if they don't know where it will lead them as Abraham's life shows.
5. God calls his people to believe him for miracles as Sarah did.
6. The Lord asks his people to accept tests of faith and love to develop their relationship with him as Abraham did.

"This is the faith-path being developed by God for the *remnant* to follow in keeping with God's *covenant*."

Chapter 8

The Self-Centered Path

Isaac stepped out of his tent and looked to the northern horizon. It has been months since Eliezer my father's servant left to go to the region of Haran to find a bride for me, he mused. I see a little movement. Could this be the camels coming? Calm down heart. I can hardly catch my breath. Yes, the camels are coming. Why are they moving so slowly? I can hardly wait. I would like to run to meet them, but that hardly seems appropriate. Plus, I don't know if Eliezer has been successful in finding a bride for me.

The camels are still a long way off, but I think I can make out the form of a lady. Yes. I see her. Well, I did. She just covered her face with a veil. Will those camels ever get here?

"The bride God has chosen for you, Master," said Eliezer as the camel knelt to the ground. Isaac grasped the damsel's left hand with his right hand and swung his left arm around her back to help her step from the carriage on the beast's back.

"Come to my tent, dear one. Now let me lift your veil. How beautiful you are. What is your name?"

"Rebekah," she whispered with eyes aglow.

They were married and twins were born.

Foresight

~

"This stone is not the most comfortable pillow I ever slept on," said Jacob to himself as he settled down to sleep for the night along the path to Haran. Eventually, sleep came.

A ladder reached from the earth to heaven. Angels were climbing up and down it. And from the top of the ladder the Lord said:

> "I am the Lord, the God of Abraham your father and the God of Isaac. The land on which you lie I will give to you and to your offspring. Your offspring shall be like the dust of the earth, and you shall spread abroad to the west and to the east and to the north and to the south, and in you and your offspring shall all the families of the earth be blessed. Behold, I am with you and will keep you wherever you go, and will bring you back to this land. For I will not leave you until I have done what I have promised you" (Genesis 28:13-15).

Jacob awoke and said, "I was feeling so alone, having to flee from my home to avoid Esau's intentions to kill me for supplanting him out of the birthright. But now I know God is with me." Then he declared:

> "If God will be with me and will keep me in this way that I go, and will give me bread to eat and clothing to wear, so that I come again to my father's house in peace, then the Lord shall be my God" (Genesis 28:20-21).

~

Jacob slumped on the fallen log by the well, his travel-worn clothes hanging over his drooped shoulders and heavy heart. The memory of home gnawed at his spirit. Some friendly-looking men approached, but he was in no mood for company.

"Good day, sir. You must be new to this area?"

"Yes, I come from the far South. Where are you from?"

"Right over here in Haran." One of them pointed toward the

The Self-Centered Path

North.

Jacob jumped to his feet, his eyes wide. "That is the place I am looking for. I had no idea I was so close to my destination. Do you know Laban, the son of Nahor?"

"Certainly. Oh look. His daughter is coming with her sheep."

But Jacob's gaze was already on her. What sparkling eyes! What exquisite lips! What flawless, light bronze skin!

"Why do we stand here waiting instead of removing the stone from the well's mouth so people can water their sheep?" Jacob asked.

"Can't you see? The stone is heavy. Besides, it is our daily custom to wait until everyone is—"

Not waiting to hear more, Jacob leaped forward and grabbed the edge of the stone cover. With muscles bulging he flipped the huge stone off of the well all by himself. Then he drew water and filled the trough before Rachel's sheep.

While the sheep drank, Rachel said nothing, but her gaze fixed on Jacob. What a muscular physique. What a finely chiseled face. And this man does not feel it is beneath him to water my sheep. What a guy! Their eyes met. Jacob approached and drew her to himself.

"I am your father's sister's son," he announced, as he kissed her on the cheek.

Rachel felt her heart pounding as a strange warmth filled her body. Terrified, she broke free and ran to tell her father that a cousin was at the well.

How foolish of me, thought Jacob, again I have blown a good thing. Why was I so impetuous? I didn't have to hug and kiss the maiden the moment I met her. Well, her sheep are still here. Someone will come for them. I will wait.

Again, the memories of home flooded back, There too I was impatient. Of course, my mother Rebekah didn't help. She insisted that I dress in my brother's hunting clothes, put goats' hair on my arms and neck, and go to my father and ask for the blessing.

Foresight

~

Rebekah gave birth to twin boys. The first one was very hairy and came out with his smooth brother grasping his heel. She named the first son Esau, meaning rough, and the second son Jacob, meaning heel grabber or supplanter.

The rough, hairy one grew up outdoors with the wind in his face, learning the stealth of a hunter and how to shoot arrows straight to their target.

The heel-grabber grew up staying at home and learning how to grab his mother's love to himself, away from his brother. His mother idolized him and wanted him to have the best of everything, even at Esau's expense. Consequently, neither she nor Jacob could bear the thought of Esau having the family birthright even though the firstborn was normally entitled to it. The birthright was a special blessing from the father. It made the person who received it the family leader and controller of the family wealth.

Isaac was old and he had commissioned Esau to prepare a venison meal for the blessing ceremony. But when Esau went to the field to hunt a deer, Jacob did the deceptive act. His nearly- blind, aged father smelled Esau's deer-scented clothes in which Rebekah had dressed Jacob. Isaac felt the goats' hair on Jacob's arms. Jacob felt and smelled like Esau, so Isaac blessed Jacob, believing he blessed Esau.

~

Yes, my act enraged Esau so I had to flee my brother's intent to kill me, recalled Jacob. He stared down the path of Rachel's flight, longing to see her reappear. Eventually a man on a dead run appeared on the path. Moments later Jacob felt his warm embrace.

Rachel's father Laban said, "You are my relative, bone of my bone and flesh of my flesh. Come home with me. Tell me of my sister

The Self-Centered Path

and your father Isaac. Tell me all. It's been a long time since I have heard from them."

After Jacob had lived and worked for a month with Laban, Laban said to him, "Just because you're my relative, should you work for me for nothing? Tell me what your wages should be."

Jacob responded, "Well, I am really in love with Rachel, but as you know I am now separated from my family's wealth. What if I work seven years as dowry for her?"

"It is a deal," said Laban.

Time flew by. After seven years Laban threw a wedding and Jacob married the veiled bride. But the next morning he discovered that his new wife was not the beautiful Rachel but her homely sister Leah.

"What have you done to me, Laban?" Jacob demanded, "I will not accept this trickery."

"You should have known that the oldest daughter always marries first," said Laban. "But don't worry. You can marry Rachel next week. Of course, you will have to work another seven years for her."

Jacob's hard work made Laban's sheep business prosper. At the end of the fourteen years Laban was eager for Jacob to stay on.

Jacob said to him, "I will work for you on a partnership basis. From now on you will give me all the existing speckled, spotted, and streaked sheep and goats. Also, from now on you will give me all the lambs and kids born with these marks. On these conditions, I will continue to tend your flocks along with mine."

"Agreed," said Laban, with an inward grin. This was really a good deal. What could Jacob be thinking?

Jacob's livestock operation was far from Laban's watchful eye. This allowed Jacob to do some things on the sly. He cut notches through the bark of tree branches to expose the color of the wood inside. He put these branches in the ewe's watering troughs, believing it would make the ewes birth spotted offspring. He also engaged in

Foresight

selective breeding by having the speckled, spotted, and black males breed the females. The result was female sheep and goats giving birth to speckled, spotted, and black offspring. By this means Jacob grew large flocks from Laban's flocks.

Over the next few years Laban and his sons saw much of the family animal wealth go to Jacob. They grew hostile to him. Jacob felt threatened. So gathering his family, his flocks, and all his other wealth, he started on a journey back home. He would go back to the land of his fathers, to the land God had promised his grandfather Abraham.

After months of travel, when the Jacob entourage finally drew near to their destination, Jacob became fearful of how Esau would receive him. He sent messengers ahead with large gifts of sheep and goats to meet Esau.

Chapter 9

Full Surrender

The angels stood directly ahead of Jacob, silently blocking his path.[12] What is this about? mused the startled Jacob. Well it reminds me of the last time I saw angels. Yes, I was on my journey to Haran twenty years ago, the land I just left. I stopped one night to sleep on the ground with a stone for my pillow. I dreamed of angels climbing up and down a ladder from earth to heaven. And God spoke some promises to me which were obviously conditional on whether I would serve him.

Well, I now recognize God is here again, God is getting my attention. The angels do not speak, but by their gaze I know they are reminding me of the promise I made back then when I said,

"If God will be with me and will keep me in this way that I go, and will give me bread to eat and clothing to wear, so that I come again to my father's house in peace, then the Lord shall be my God" (Genesis 28:20-21).

---

[12] See Genesis 32:1

Foresight

I promised this in response to the covenant God offered me, Jacob continued to ponder. I get it. The Lord wants to confirm the covenant he offered me those twenty years ago according to the promise I made then. Wow! I sure have a way of locking myself into situations. I just got free from servitude to Laban, caused by a rash promise. Now I am faced with the consequences of another rash promise. I really do want to regard the God of my fathers, but am I ready to fully surrender and commit to him?"

The angels gradually faded from his view. But immediately another sight got his attention. The messengers he had sent to Esau came running to him. "Esau is on his way with an army of four hundred armed men," they cried out.

Jacob's face went white and a tremor shot up his spine. The day of reckoning has come, he thought. Jacob sent his family and flocks with their shepherds over the brook ahead. As it grew dark, he imagined that Esau, or one of the angels he had just seen, would bound out of the shadows any minute now. And they would strike him a death blow.

A movement in the bushes. A human form burst forth. Instantly, with his mind racing, Jacob leaped upon the man to wrestle him to the ground. I, Jacob, the one who always wins any contest, will not be defeated. Not now when I and my family are so close to home. I outwitted my treacherous father-in-law, supplanted my brother, and tricked my own father to win. I will not give way to defeat now.

But this man will not go down. In fact, he seems to play with me, resisting my struggle just enough to spend my energy. Through the night they wrestled. The more Jacob struggled the more desperate he became. Finally, the man struck Jacob and dislocated his hip. For the first time in his life, Jacob was at the mercy of his opponent, bereft of any strategy to recover his loss. Yet strangely an inexplicable peace spread over him.

Who is this admirable man of such strength and endurance? If only I could be like Him in this my hour of need.

He clung to the God-Man as the truth dawned: He was wrestling

Full Surrender

with God. Oh how I need God at this moment of total vulnerability, bereft of all self-sufficiency!

> Then he said, "Let me go, for the day has broken."
> But Jacob said, "I will not let you go unless you bless me."
> And he said to him, "What is your name?"
> And he said, "Jacob" (Genesis 32:26-27).

"Oh, what confession there is in your name!" the God-man continued. "You have been the self-centered heel grabber, exemplifying the meaning of your name, Jacob. Your life has been about greedily grabbing all you can get at others' expense. It is right for you to persevere in life, but it is not right for you to win through craftiness and deceit and at others' expense. The only way to really win is to do things God's way—in His strength—not your own."

> Then he said, "Your name shall no longer be called Jacob, but Israel, for you have striven with God and with men, and have prevailed" (Genesis 32:28).

"Yes, Lord. Through my defeat in wrestling you I have won the greatest battle ever. I now see myself as inadequate. I could have gotten what I needed in my past life through depending on you instead of my self-centered schemes. Now I feel my desperate need of you. Please tell me your name."

"Why do you ask what my name is? You will know me by the blessing I now give you."

The Spirit of the Lord moved over Jacob in waves of joy. Intense love for his Lord and others flooded his heart. *Faith* pervaded and dominated his intellect in place of the old prideful self-dependency. No longer would his life be all about what material things he could own and experience. He would not live just to pleasure his senses instead of finding the joy of the Lord through prayer and fellowship with his Maker.

He acknowledged to himself, "I now know that God is more important to me than anything else. I will cling to the Lord the rest of

Foresight

my life. I will *hope* in him. No more will I be all about placing my hope in material things. No longer will I be grasping for all the sheep and goats and other *material* wealth I can acquire. I will trust God and live out my *faith* in my life. My life will be centered in God instead of myself. And yes, I will keep the promise I made to God twenty years ago."

~

It was morning and Jacob had gotten no sleep, but he crossed over the brook and said to his family, "We must go to meet my brother."

When the sun was still low in the eastern sky, Esau and his four hundred men appeared over the knoll just ahead. Jacob hobbled forward on his injured hip and bowed to the ground before Esau.

Seeing this, Esau realized, I have no reason to be afraid of this broken, humble man.

He ran to meet Jacob. He hugged and kissed his brother. Then they wept together in the spirit of brotherly love.

Jacob introduced his family to Esau and then proclaimed, "I have a lot to tell you about the last twenty years."

"And I also have a few things to tell you, my brother." Esau replied.

The all-day, intense conversation finally ended late in the night when the brothers were exhausted. Then Jacob announced to his family, "Tomorrow we will continue our journey to the land of Canaan where we will live out the life of promise God has for us. I am so anxious to see my father. He has instilled in me a vision of building a future with God."

* * *

"Yes! Yes!" said Gabriel standing nearby. "Even though Isaac

Full Surrender

blessed Jacob by mistake, God honored the blessing as we see in Jacob's life. God also blessed Esau, though he was not considered a person of faith. Biblical history will show Isaac's and Jacob's faith in this statement:

And those things involved a full submission and commitment to God.
  "Let's review the faith-path with Isaac and Jacob added:
1. God requires people to place faith in a blood sacrifice as Abel's actions show.
2. God calls people to focus on pleasing him as Enoch did.
3. God calls his followers to focus on saving their families from the destruction of sin as did Noah.
4. The Lord calls his people to come out from idolatry and follow his leadership, even if they don't know where it will lead them as Abraham's life shows.
5. God calls his people to believe him for miracles as Sarah did.
6. The LORD asks his people to accept tests of faith and love to develop their relationship with him as Abraham did.
7. God calls his people to surrender and commit fully to him as Isaac and Jacob did.

"Yes. This is the faith-path being developed by God for the *remnant* to follow in keeping his *covenant*."

* * *

"Well, that was not what we were working for. I thought we had Esau programmed to kill Jacob on his first sight of him," yelled Satan. "It has been bad enough to watch Abraham escape Sumer. It was even worse to see Abraham and Isaac develop hopes of building a godly nation designed to defeat our efforts to bring people to *despair*. We did get our clutches on Esau through giving him a passion for sensual, instant gratification. His *sensualism* was in full control of his life. This was evident when he sold his birthright to Jacob for the sensory pleasure of a bowl of soup. I didn't like the idea of anyone getting a birthright to help him promote God's cause. But I thought Jacob would use it for his own earthly gain.

"His prideful *humanistic* way of getting ahead of God by using deceit instead of trusting God seemed to guarantee this. He was indifferent toward God the whole time he was in Haran. When we used Laban to trick him, I thought he would blame God and turn against the Creator. This didn't happen, but when the family started out to return to Canaan Jacob's heart was still cold toward the Lord."

"Yes," said An. "Even though the Abraham family got out of Sumer from its idol worshiping snare, Jacob was worshiping himself, idolizing himself and riches. He seemed to be just as ensnared, and on his way to total *despair* as much as the idol worshipers of Sumer.

"How could we know that God would use our *despair* program to bring him to the end of himself? How could we know he would throw all of his care on God and begin to trust him with a *faith* as strong as Abraham's? And then how could we know that the LORD would touch the heart of Esau to embrace his brother instead of killing him? Satan, I am beginning to agree with Aga. You cannot win against God. He is playing you like a harp. The Lord uses what you mean for evil to accomplish good."

"Hold on here, An. This is all your fault. I put you in charge of idol worship. You not only let the Abraham family out of Sumer; you failed to keep Jacob in Haran away from the Promised Land."

All the demons glared at Satan with bared teeth. He glared back. His whole being wrenched and writhed as a reddish hue rose up through his black face. He opened his mouth to shout more venom but then thought he better not. Now was not the time.

Instead the devil put on a plastic smile and said, "We must live and learn. Better days are coming. We will see how committed God's

Full Surrender

people are to him when we turn them into groveling slaves. The bondage will drive them to *despair* of ever being on the winning side of life again and make them lose all hope in the Lord."

The imps only continued to glare and snarl at Satan, but with even more animosity.

Foresight

Chapter 10

Delivered

"We've got them now," cried Satan rubbing his hands together in hellish glee. "Getting Israel and his family from their land of promise to Egypt has been a long process. Now we can really bring our program of *despair* to bear on them and seriously deplete their faith, love and hope. Getting Leah's sons to sell their half-brother, Joseph the son of Rachel, into Egypt as a slave was sweet revenge on God. Seeing Joseph's brothers pour out their hatred on him really filled us with glee, not joy. For joy is the fruit of God's Spirit, and we aren't privy to such. Perversion and hatred are our fruit. And I have an abundance of it.

"I know the Lord thinks he has brought good from what we meant for evil by our conniving to get Joseph sold into slavery. And I admit I am not a bit happy to see Joseph sitting on the Egyptian throne as the prime minister of the land. His faithfulness to God in his great adversity led him from slavery to this. But the win for us was seeing the Jacob family leave the Promised Land and go to Egypt after they reconnected with Joseph. This paves the way for the Egyptians to eventually put them in bondage. Yet it really gripes me to know that we might have to be patient until Joseph and the present good-hearted Pharaoh die for this to happen. But then we can drive

Foresight

the next Pharaoh to gradually dominate and intimidate the Israelites until their spirits are broken."

* * *

"Oh yes, Satan. If you were as smart as you claim, you would have done things differently," said Michael for only Gabriel to hear. "Joseph has been faithful through everything you put him through. You corrupted Jacob for a time and corrupted his children, but Joseph and a few who stand with him make up a *remnant* that are determined to keep *covenant* with God. Joseph never forgot where he came from and the promise tied to the land. Biblical history will record Joseph's outstanding faith with these words:

> " By faith Joseph, at the end of his life, made mention of the exodus of the Israelites and gave directions concerning his bones" (Hebrews 11:22).

Gabriel smiled broadly, "This adds one more development to the faith-path:

1. God requires people to place faith in a blood sacrifice as Abel's actions show.
2. God calls people to focus on pleasing him as Enoch did.
3. God calls his followers to focus on saving their families from the destruction of sin as did Noah.
4. The Lord calls his people to come out from idolatry and follow his leadership, even if they don't know where it will lead them as Abraham's life shows.
5. God calls his people to believe him for miracles as Sarah did.
6. The Lord asks his people to accept tests of faith and love to develop their relationship with him as Abraham did.
7. God calls his people to surrender and commit fully to him as Isaac and Jacob did.
8. God leads the faithful to never lose sight of the land of promise

Delivered

following Joseph's example.

"Yes. This is the faith-path being developed by God for the *remnant* to follow in keeping his *covenant*."

~

> Now there arose a new king over Egypt, who did not know Joseph. And he said to his people, "Behold, the people of Israel are too many and too mighty for us. Come, let us deal shrewdly with them, lest they multiply, and, if war breaks out, they join our enemies and fight against us and escape from the land." Therefore they set taskmasters over them to afflict them with heavy burdens. They built for Pharaoh store cities, Pithom and Raamses (Exodus 1:8-11).

The children of Israel built the cities of Pithom and Rameses for Pharaoh. The harder their taskmasters made them work in brick and mortar the more they multiplied. And the more they multiplied the harder the Egyptians worked them.

But the Lord heard the cry of his people in this awful bondage and sent Moses to Pharaoh to say to him, "Let my people Israel go."

Pharaoh leaned forward and rubbed his chin. He lowered his eyelids and looked through his eyelashes. "Who is this God who dares to ask me to let our slaves go from serving us?" demanded Pharaoh.

"You shall soon know," said Moses as he returned Pharaoh's glare with his own intense stare as he stroked his beard.

The drinking water turned into blood. Pharaoh sneered, "I won't take this to heart. We will survive."

The frogs came croaking out of the Nile into the beds, ovens, and kneading bowls. The king frowned. Then he scowled. More frogs came and his face turned angry-red. They crawled into his bed and his face turned sick-white. Finally, he cried, "Get those rascals, Moses and Aaron, back here."

"These plagues are kind of inconvenient. I will let the miserable slaves go."

Foresight

"When?" asked Moses

"Oh, tomorrow."

"Tomorrow it will be."

"Well, I guess I have changed my mind," said Pharaoh.

The dust turned to pesky gnats at the swing of Aaron's rod. Thick swarms of flies crawled into the Egyptians' eyes, noses, and ears.

"Moses, your people can go, but not too far."

"Oh. I see the flies are now gone. I have decided not to let you go. Why should I let my slaves go?"

The Egyptians' livestock began to die in droves. Aaron threw furnace dust into boils on man and animals. Huge hail stones fell with blinding lightning from the sky.

Pharaoh sent for Moses and Aaron. "I have sinned this time," he said to them. "The Lord is the righteous one, and I and my people are the guilty ones. Make an appeal to the Lord. There has been enough of God's thunder and hail. I will let you go. You don't need to stay any longer."

Pharaoh reneged, "No. I didn't really mean that. Things seem to be all right now. Your people will stay after all, Moses."

Locusts ate up all the plants and the fruit on the trees.

Pharaoh caved again. He said, "Yes."

When the locusts were gone, he said, "No."

The sun refused to shine, and the darkness was so intense one couldn't see his hand in front of his face.

"Yes. You can go."

"But the darkness is now gone. No. You may not go."

The more the plagues came, the harder Pharaoh's heart became. Red-faced, and eyes glaring, he shouted to Moses:

"Leave me! Make sure you never see my face again, for on the day you see my face, you will die" (Exodus 10:28).

"As you have declared," Moses replied. "I will never see your face again" (Exodus 10:28-29).

Delivered

~

"I sense something is wrong and it is still night. Let me go check on the children," said Pharaoh's wife to Pharaoh.

"Our firstborn son is not breathing. Oh no! He is dead!" she wailed.

The attendant next door cried, "Our son is dead. Oh no! Our son doesn't respond."

The wails rose throughout the night. Every home with children found the oldest child dead. "Get those children of Israel out of here. We will all be dead. Hurry. Hurry. Please get out of our land," cried the Egyptians. "We will all be dead if you don't leave!"

"Give us your gold and clothes," replied the Israelites.

"Here take our gold rings, our silver bracelets, our head bands, our cloaks. Here. Take these. Here. Here. Take all of these valuable items. Take them one. Take them all."

~

"We are on our way! We are on our way!" shouted the descendants of Israel. "Our cattle and your precious metals and other possessions go with us."

With steady pace, in a few days they were at the Red Sea. But when they looked back, they saw dust rising in the direction they had just left. There were the Egyptians coming after them.

> And the people of Israel cried out to the Lord. They said to Moses, "Is it because there are no graves in Egypt that you have taken us away to die in the wilderness? What have you done to us in bringing us out of Egypt? Is not this what we said to you in Egypt: 'Leave us alone that we may serve the Egyptians'? For it would have been better for us to serve the Egyptians than to die in the wilderness."

Foresight

> And Moses said to the people, "Fear not, stand firm, and see the salvation of the Lord, which he will work for you today. For the Egyptians whom you see today, you shall never see again. The Lord will fight for you, and you have only to be silent" (Exodus 14:10-14).

An Angel in a cloud of the Lord's presence had been going before his people. Now the angel and the cloud moved behind them to block the vision of the Egyptians. Their pursuers could no longer see ahead to pursue, because the side of the cloud before them was darkness. But the side facing the Israelites was a fiery light to light up the night for them.

Moses pointed his staff over the sea. The Lord sent a powerful east wind all that night. The wind blew the water to the left and the right and the riverbed turned into a dry road. The Israelites marched through between the walls of water.

"Aha," cried the armored Egyptians. "We can do that too." Drivers cracked their whips. Horses leaned into their harnesses. Chariot wheels whirled their way into the sea.

Looking over their shoulders to see the slave masters coming at them, the Lord's people cried, "Let's go. Let's go!" Never did such a large assembly move so fast on foot.

"The path is becoming soft," cried one Egyptian.

"My wheels are getting stuck in the mud," lamented another.

"We're bogging down."

"We're sinking deeper and deeper into the mud."

"Why were we so headstrong and stupid? The God of Israel is fighting for them."

"Oh, what is our hard-hearted, hard-headed Pharaoh going to do for us now?"

"Look! Water is flowing toward us. Run!"

"Run. Run."

"Run! Run! Run!"

Delivered

God's people were now on the shore, out of the seabed. Moses pointed his staff back toward the Egyptians. Instantly, the walls of water crumbled and came crashing down on all the king's horses and all the king's men. As the Israelites stood on the shore someone said, "Look. Our slave masters' dead bodies are floating on the water, drifting toward us."

The people shuddered at the sight, but then broke out in praise:

> "I will sing to the Lord, for he has triumphed gloriously;
>   the horse and his rider he has thrown into the sea.
> The Lord is my strength and my song,
>   and he has become my salvation;
> this is my God, and I will praise him,
> my father's God, and I will exalt him.
> The Lord is a man of war;
>   the Lord is his name.
> "Pharaoh's chariots and his host he cast into the sea,
> and his chosen officers were sunk in the Red Sea.
> The floods covered them;
>   they went down into the depths like a stone.
> Your right hand, O Lord, glorious in power,
>   your right hand, O Lord, shatters the enemy" (Exodus 15:1-6).

* * *

"Why did God allow his people to become slaves for so long and then bring about this great deliverance?" asked Gabriel.

"God intended to saturate the memories of the Israelites with the realization that sin enslaves people and faith in him delivers them," answered Michael. "Even though God used Joseph's presence in Egypt for good, the brothers meant it for evil. This resulted in their going to Egypt where they fell into slavery. Their memory of the hard,

Foresight

miserable bondage in slavery should always keep them focused on following God and doing what is right."

Chapter 11

The Ten Commandments

Several days after leaving Egypt, the Israelites arrived at Mt. Sinai. They settled in and camped there. Then the Lord made himself known to them. Thunder clapped and lightning lit up the mountain. Trumpet sounds blasted the air waves. Everyone in the camp shuddered.

Yet Moses commanded all the people to go forth to the foot of the mountain to meet God—even as the mountain shook violently and smoke billowed all around it. The shaking continued as the trumpet sounded louder and louder.

God came down to the top of the mountain and called Moses to come up to him. But when he got there, God sent him back down to warn the people not to come close to the mountain. Then God proclaimed:

"I am the Lord your God, who brought you out of the land of Egypt, out of the house of slavery.

"You shall have no other gods before me.

Foresight

"You shall not make for yourself a carved image, or any likeness of anything that is in heaven above, or that is in the earth beneath, or that is in the water under the earth. You shall not bow down to them or serve them, for I the Lord your God am a jealous God, visiting the iniquity of the fathers on the children to the third and the fourth generation of those who hate me, 6 but showing steadfast love to thousands of those who love me and keep my commandments.

"You shall not take the name of the Lord your God in vain, for the Lord will not hold him guiltless who takes his name in vain.

"Remember the Sabbath day, to keep it holy. Six days you shall labor, and do all your work, but the seventh day is a Sabbath to the Lord your God. On it you shall not do any work, you, or your son, or your daughter, your male servant, or your female servant, or your livestock, or the sojourner who is within your gates. For in six days the Lord made heaven and earth, the sea, and all that is in them, and rested on the seventh day. Therefore the Lord blessed the Sabbath day and made it holy.

"Honor your father and your mother, that your days may be long in the land that the Lord your God is giving you.

"You shall not murder.

"You shall not commit adultery.

"You shall not steal.

"You shall not bear false witness against your neighbor.

"You shall not covet your neighbor's house; you shall not covet your neighbor's wife, or his male servant, or his female servant, or his ox, or his donkey, or anything that is your neighbor's" (Exodus 20:2-17).

The people were afraid and trembled, and they stood far off [19] and said to Moses, "You speak to us, and we will listen; but do not let God speak to us, lest we die."

Ten Commandments

> Moses said to the people, "Do not fear, for God has come to test you, that the fear of him may be before you, that you may not sin" (Exodus 20:19 -20).

The people stood at a distance as Moses and a young man named Joshua climbed the mountain.

Joshua observed, "You know, Moses, the first four of the commandments are about love for God and the last six are about love of fellow people."

"A very astute observation, my son," replied Moses. This shows that God intends to advance his agenda through love.

* * *

Above the mountain, Gabriel peered at the scene with flaming eyes. "How fascinating is this?"

"I cannot wait to see what this is all about!" declared Michael with eyes all aglow. They watched as God gave Moses tablets of stone on which he had written the Ten Commandments.

"Oh. I see," whispered Gabriel. "God has given Moses a hard copy of the commandments he proclaimed from the mountaintop."

"Yes," replied Michael. "These commandments are the terms and conditions, assigned to God's people for keeping their part of the *covenant*."

* * *

The Lord introduced Moses to a plan to have continual, daily sacrifice. This would come to be known as the Tamid, for tamid is the Hebrew word for "standing" or "continual." Tamid would consist of offering an unblemished lamb with grain mixed with oil from crushed olives. One such offering would be offered in the morning and one in

Foresight

the evening, at the ninth hour[13] at 3 p.m. The fire burning these sacrifices would burn all day and all night continually. Fire would be burning on the altar at all times.

God also gave Moses precise instructions on how to build a tent to be God's dwelling. There the priests would offer the Tamid and other sacrifices to him. This tent was to have two rooms separated by a curtain. One room would be called the holy place and the other would be called the most holy place. The tent would be surrounded by a court with cloth walls. Within this court on a large altar in front of the tabernacle the Tamid lambs would be offered. Their blood would be taken to an incense altar in the holy place where it would be mixed with burning incense to create smoke. The smoke would represent the people reaching up to God and him accepting their offering. This created a sense of developing relationship with God.

God also told Moses to keep yearly feasts and offer sacrifices at those feasts. One feast be the Feast of Passover to celebrate the night the Israelites left Egypt after the death angel passed over and saved the firstborn of the Israelites. Another would be the Feast of Weeks, or Pentecost, to celebrate the first fruits of harvest. It would also celebrate the giving of the Ten Commandments and other laws on Mt. Sinai. A third would be the Feast of Tabernacles to celebrate the end of harvest and God's continual provision for his people.

* * *

Michael observed, "The daily sacrifice and all of these feasts will embody a promise, which we don't fully understand. But they will foreshadow a time when the sacrifices—which are only tokens of a greater sacrifice needed—will be redeemed, removing the need

---

[13] Josephus, Antiquities of the Jews, 14.4.3

Ten Commandments

for animal sacrifices."

"I assume you gained all this knowledge from the Book of Truth," Gabriel clarified.

"Yes. Indeed I did. Now it is time to review the developments of the faith-path Moses made as the Bible will record:

> "By faith Moses, when he was born, was hidden for three months by his parents, because they saw that the child was beautiful, and they were not afraid of the king's edict.
>
> "By faith Moses, when he was grown up, refused to be called the son of Pharaoh's daughter, choosing rather to be mistreated with the people of God than to enjoy the fleeting pleasures of sin. He considered the reproach of Christ greater wealth than the treasures of Egypt, for he was looking to the reward. By faith he left Egypt, not being afraid of the anger of the king, for he endured as seeing him who is invisible.
>
> "By faith he kept the Passover and sprinkled the blood, so that the Destroyer of the firstborn might not touch them.
>
> "By faith the people crossed the Red Sea as on dry land, but the Egyptians, when they attempted to do the same, were drowned." (Hebrews 11:23-29).

"Let's review the faith-path and add Moses' contribution to it," insisted Gabriel.

1. God requires people to place faith in a blood sacrifice as Abel's actions show.
2. He calls people to focus on pleasing him as Enoch did.
3. God calls his followers to focus on saving their families from the destruction of sin as did Noah.
4. The Lord calls his people to come out from idolatry and follow his leadership, even if they don't know where it will lead them as Abraham's life shows.
5. God calls his people to believe him for miracles as Sarah did.
6. The Lord asks his people to accept tests of faith and love to

Foresight

      develop their relationship with him as Abraham did.
7. God calls his people to surrender and commit fully to him as Isaac and Jacob did.
8. God leads the faithful to never lose sight of the land of promise following Joseph's example.
9. God calls his people to trust him to part their Red Sea to a spiritual, sacrificial life of commitment to him as Moses did rather than pursuing sensory pleasures of the world.

      "Yes. This is the faith-path being developed by God for the *remnant* to follow in keeping with God's *covenant*."

Chapter 12

Conquering the Promised Land

The two Israelite spies who had entered Jericho of Canaan to case it out promised, "We will spare you and any of your family who are in your house because you hid us from those who came for us. But you must hang this rope out of your window. This way every Israelite will know this house is to be protected."

Rahab the prostitute agreed: "Since you are in my house on the city wall, I can let you down outside our city from my window with this scarlet rope. And when I see your army coming, I will hang this same rope out of this window so you will know this is my house and will not destroy it."

~

Canaan was filled with people following the false way of Satan. This made them seriously evil to the very core of their souls. Their fertility religion promoted all kinds of sexual immorality plus witchcraft and child sacrifice.

Foresight

> A bronze image of Kronos was set up among them, stretching out its cupped hands above a bronze cauldron, which would burn the child. As the flame burning the child surrounded the body, the limbs would shrivel up and the mouth would appear to grin as if laughing, until it was shrunk enough to slip into the cauldron.[14]

~

A million-plus descendants of Israel stood outside the walled city of Jericho with its gates securely barred against their entrance. Who was this man standing before them with his sword drawn?

Joshua approached him and asked,

"Are you for us or for our enemies?"

"Neither," He replied. "I have now come as commander of the Lord's army."

Then Joshua bowed with his face to the ground in worship and asked him, "What does my Lord want to say to His servant?"

"Take off your sandals from your feet, for the place where you are standing is holy." And Joshua did so (Joshua 5:14-15).

The next day, the Lord said to Joshua:

"See, I have given Jericho into your hand, with its king and mighty men of valor. You shall march around the city, all the men of war going around the city once. Thus shall you do for six days. Seven priests shall bear seven trumpets of rams' horns before the ark. On the seventh day you shall march around the city seven times, and the priests shall blow the trumpets. And when they make a long blast with the ram's horn, when you hear the sound of the trumpet, then all the people shall shout with a great shout, and the wall of the city will fall down flat, and the people shall go up, everyone straight before him" (Joshua 6:2-5).

---

[14] https,//www.str.org/publications/the-canaanites-genocide-or-judgment#_edn12

Conquering the Promised Land

The people followed these instructions every day. On the seventh day, very early in the morning, soldiers and priests marched around Jericho the first time, the second time, the third time, and again, until the seventh time. The marchers came to the finish line. The priests blasted loud and long with their trumpets.

All the soldiers, with the people standing by, shouted a miraculously loud, thunderous roar. The earth trembled. The walls of the city-state began to vibrate and shake. Cracks appeared, then wide breaks. The walls crumbled in a billowing cloud of dust.

This was the beginning. City-state after city-state fell before the Israelites' attack. The people possessed the land.

God's people lived in abundance in the Promised Land with Joshua as their leader. When he was getting ready to pass on, he assembled the people. He then challenged them to keep covenant with God. He declared:

> If you forsake the Lord and serve foreign gods, then he will turn and do you harm and consume you, after having done you good."
>
> And the people said to Joshua, "No, but we will serve the Lord."
>
> Then Joshua said to the people, "You are witnesses against yourselves that you have chosen the Lord, to serve him."
>
> And they said, "We are witnesses."
>
> He said, "Then put away the foreign gods that are among you, and incline your heart to the Lord, the God of Israel" (Joshua 24:20-23).

* * *

"Oh yes," proclaimed Gabriel. "This confirms what we have been thinking: Joshua clearly has shown that God's covenant is conditional. God can only keep *covenant* with the *remnant* who keep

Foresight

the conditions of his covenant. And the people have confirmed they know this by insisting they will keep their part of the covenant. They understand that God will turn against them and destroy them if they fail to keep covenant with God."

"Yes, Gabriel. This gives us another development for the faith-path," declared Michael. "Biblical history will record it with these words,

> "By faith the walls of Jericho fell down after they had been encircled for seven days.
> "By faith Rahab the prostitute did not perish with those who were disobedient, because she had given a friendly welcome to the spies" (Hebrews 11:30-31).

"Let's review the faith-path with Rahab added.

1. God requires people to place faith in a blood sacrifice as Abel's actions show.
2. God calls people to focus on pleasing him as Enoch did.
3. God calls his followers to focus on saving their families from the destruction of sin as did Noah.
4. The Lord calls his people to come out from idolatry and follow his leadership, even if they don't know where it will lead them as Abraham's life shows.
5. God calls his people to believe him for miracles as Sarah did.
6. The Lord asks his people to accept tests of faith and love to develop their relationship with him as Abraham did.
7. God calls his people to surrender and commit fully to him as Isaac and Jacob did.
8. God leads the faithful to never lose sight of the land of promise following Joseph's example.
9. God calls his people to trust him to part their Red Sea, to a spiritual, sacrificial life of commitment to him as Moses did rather than pursuing sensory pleasures of the world.
10. God calls his saints to trust him to break down the walls of

falsehood which stand in the way of truth as the Israelites trusted God to break down the walls of Jericho.
11. God calls the world to align themselves with God's cause as Rahab did.

"Yes. This is the faith-path being developed by God for the *remnant* to follow in keeping his *covenant*."

Foresight

Chapter 13

Earthly Kingdom Inaugurated

"This just won't do," pronounced Satan. "If God succeeds in keeping Israel separated from the world our cause is lost. How absolutely deplorable. Only through worldly people can we advance the deadly -isms of worldliness. We must infiltrate the Lord's people with these -isms, our perverted forms of faith, hope, and love. As much as I hate to admit the horrible reality, we cannot create anything, but we sure enough can corrupt and pervert. We can pervert *faith* into *pride-of-life humanism*, inordinate self-dependency. We can pervert *love* into *lust-of-the-flesh sensualism*, the obsessive love of pleasure. Oh yes. And we can pervert *hope* into *lust-of-the-eyes materialism*, being preoccupied with material things.

"Yes. Yes. Our -isms are the counterintelligence falsehoods capable of counteracting the truth dynamics of love, hope, and faith. But to open the Israelites' hearts to this false way, we must break down their commitment to trusting God like I did with Eve in the Garden. That victory was sweet. We must incite them to think they need a human king—a human being to trust who has a tangible,

Foresight

physical presence in their midst. We can do this by introducing the *humanistic* counterintelligence idea that God is too far away and abstract.

"This will get them well on their way to trusting in the arm of flesh. Then we will take control of the king. But first we will let him prosper and drive the people to a cult-fascination with their human representative. He will swell with pride until he feels like a god. This will drive him to compel people to look only to him for leadership instead of following God's directions from Samuel. Ah. This is going to be almost as sweet as the victory in the Garden. The king will oppress the people by taking their sons and daughters to be his servants. He will tax them into poverty. He will abuse his power and turn into a ruthless, devouring beast. *Despair* will result."

"Yes. Yes. Mighty, brilliant king of our miserable abyss. We are at your service!" cried the imps.

Satan puffed out his chest. "You are learning. You are learning. My clever demons, you are learning to respect and honor your great leader. Now get to work. Penetrate the spirits of the Israelites who tend to be driven by their own self-importance. Tactfully whisper the thought of needing to be like the nations who have their kings. Do this with sly, cautious guile. They will think the thoughts are theirs. Then they proudly proclaim and live out our false ideas."

"We are on our way, King Satan."

* * *

> All the elders of Israel gathered together and came to Samuel at Ramah and said to him, "Behold, you are old and your sons do not walk in your ways. Now appoint for us a king to judge us like all the nations." But the thing displeased Samuel when they said, "Give us a king to judge us."

Earthly Kingdom Inaugurated

> And Samuel prayed to the Lord. And the Lord said to Samuel, "Obey the voice of the people in all that they say to you, for they have not rejected you, but they have rejected me from being king over them (1 Samuel 8:4-7).

Not long after, Samuel made it known that God wanted Saul, the son of Kish, a man who stood a head taller than the other men, to be the new king. He said to the people:

> "Do you see him whom the Lord has chosen? There is none like him among all the people." And all the people shouted, "Long live the king!"
>
> Then Samuel told the people the rights and duties of the kingship, and he wrote them in a book and laid it up before the Lord. Then Samuel sent all the people away, each one to his home (1 Samuel 10:24-25).

At first Saul humbly followed God's leadership from Samuel and the Lord blessed him with victory in battles against the enemies of Israel. But gradually he grew to resent Samuel's direction as a feeling of power went to his head. He was in this attitude when the Philistines came against Israel with 3,000 iron chariots.

Saul bore a deep frown on his face. He paced back and forth and said to himself, "Where is Samuel? He told me he would be here in seven days to offer sacrifice. This was supposed to get the mind of God as to how to proceed against the Philistines. But the troops are deserting me, and he has not come.

"Who does Samuel think he is anyway... to tell me what to do? I am the king and I am responsible for making decisions to run the kingdom. It is bad enough for him to try to control me. But when he doesn't even follow through with his agreement, it is even worse. Oh, I know he could still come today. The day is not over, but I need to show Samuel who is in charge. I will put him in his place.

Bring the burnt offering and the fellowship offering."

As Saul finished the offering, Samuel appeared, his eyes ablaze.

Foresight

Brushing his gray hair tightly back over his head with both his hands, he demanded, "What have you done?"

> Saul said, "When I saw that the people were scattering from me, and that you did not come within the days appointed, and that the Philistines had mustered at Michmash, I said, 'Now the Philistines will come down against me at Gilgal, and I have not sought the favor of the Lord.' So I forced myself, and offered the burnt offering."
>
> And Samuel said to Saul, "You have done foolishly. You have not kept the command of the Lord your God, with which he commanded you. For then the Lord would have established your kingdom over Israel forever. But now your kingdom shall not continue. The Lord has sought out a man after his own heart, and the Lord has commanded him to be prince over his people, because you have not kept what the Lord commanded you" (1 Samuel 13:11-14).

Chapter 14

A Man After God's Own Heart

Samuel mourned in deep thought, If only Saul had waited just an hour longer. I was on my way to offer the sacrifice. God was testing Saul's willingness to wait on him. But he did the unthinkable and offered the sacrifice which I was supposed to offer. After that he showed only halfhearted interest in following God's will. Then gradually he became heady and proud. He was the king and no prophet like me was going to tell him what God wanted of him. I felt threatened and feared he would kill me if I crossed Him. Gradually, he began to view me as an enemy.

Samuel cried out to God, "You know Saul was humble when you chose him to be king and you blessed his leadership. He stood a head above the rest physically. The people loved him. By your anointing, his great leadership talent developed. But as the people continued to praise him, he grew rash and proud. He seemed to feel he no longer needed your direction. The people have sensed his attitude and are beginning to lose confidence in his leadership. How different things could have been."

The Lord said to Samuel, "How long will you grieve over Saul, since I have rejected him from being king over Israel? Fill your horn

Foresight

> with oil, and go. I will send you to Jesse the Bethlehemite, for I have provided for myself a king among his sons" (1 Samuel 16:1).

~

> When they came, he looked on Eliab and thought, "Surely the Lord's anointed is before him."
>
> But the Lord said to Samuel, "Do not look on his appearance or on the height of his stature, because I have rejected him. For the Lord sees not as man sees: man looks on the outward appearance, but the Lord looks on the heart."
>
> Then Jesse called Abinadab and made him pass before Samuel. And he said, "Neither has the Lord chosen this one."
>
> Then Jesse made Shammah pass by. And he said, "Neither has the Lord chosen this one."
>
> And Jesse made seven of his sons pass before Samuel. And Samuel said to Jesse, "The Lord has not chosen these." Then Samuel said to Jesse, "Are all your sons here?"
>
> And he said, "There remains yet the youngest, but behold, he is keeping the sheep." And Samuel said to Jesse, "Send and get him, for we will not sit down till he comes here."
>
> And he sent and brought him in. Now he was ruddy and had beautiful eyes and was handsome. And the Lord said, "Arise, anoint him, for this is he."
>
> Then Samuel took the horn of oil and anointed him in the midst of his brothers. And the Spirit of the Lord rushed upon David from that day forward. And Samuel rose up and went to Ramah (1 Samuel 16:6-13).

~

The male lion crouched behind the bank near the sheep as David played his harp. Suddenly the sheep began bleating in unison. David swung around from playing his harp to see the lamb in the fleeing

A Man After God's Own Heart

beast's mouth. As swift as a deer, David pursued, staff in hand. The lion turned to charge at him. David grabbed the lamb and struck the lion's head with his staff. The startled beast let go of the lamb, but then leaped at the young man.

David deftly stepped aside, grabbed the animal by the beard with his left hand, and dealt a mighty blow to his skull with the staff in his right hand. A deadly claw swung out, but David jerked back with only a scratch on his arm. The beast gasped, shuddered, thrashed; and then lay still in death.

Day after day David played his harp as he watched his beloved sheep. This day a bear suddenly charged from behind a mound and nabbed a lamb with his teeth. David reached for his sling and swiftly picked up a stone from the ground. He ran to face the creature, now rearing up on his hind feet to his full eight-foot height. The sling whirled around and around. The released stone-bullet sped directly to its target between the eyes, crushed into the skull, and slammed a deadly concussion to the brain. The predator dropped in a heap and the lamb escaped with only a few tears in his skin.

~

David ran quickly to meet the giant Philistine whom no one else was brave enough to fight. Through a translucent vision of a reared-up bear, he saw the giant standing just a little taller. And through a like vision of a lion's paw with sharp claws, he saw the warrior's sword. Yes, this human beast would be just a little more challenge than those animal beasts. His heart pounded with fearless anticipation. His soul thirsted for conquest that would honor God. His hand thrust into his bag and took out a stone. His arm whirled the sling round and round. His fingers released one of the two ropes. The highly accelerated stone smashed into the giant's skull with a powerful thud. The unconscious hunk fell on his face to the ground.

David ran to the giant, grabbed his sword, and cut off his head.

Foresight

The Philistines fled and the men of Israel and Judah pursued. They shouted in victory as they drove their spears into their enemies. The Philistines' dead bodies lay strewn all along the Shaaraim road to Gath and Ekron.

Then as the Israelite troops returned, the women came out dancing and singing:

> "Saul has struck down his thousands,
> and David his ten thousands."
>
> And Saul was very angry, and this saying displeased him. He said, "They have ascribed to David ten thousands, and to me they have ascribed thousands, and what more can he have but the kingdom?" And Saul eyed David from that day on (1 Samuel 18:7-9).

Abner, the general of Saul's army approached David. "Young man, Saul wants to see you. Come with me."

Soon David was in the king's presence. Saul said to David, "You will remain with me. The army needs a man like you. What other talents do you possess besides being a powerful stone slinger?"

"I play the lyre."

"Ah. Tomorrow you will play the instrument before me."

That night Saul awoke in a cold sweat. He had dreamed of David sitting on his throne with a crown on his head. He tossed and turned the rest of the night with troubled thoughts, *What am I going to do with this guy? Jonathan my son instantly liked him when they met. The young men soon struck up a strong friendship. This complicates things even more,* he stewed.

The morning found blurry-eyed Saul sitting at his exquisitely crafted olive wood table. He silently stared off into the distance with a troubled frown on his face.

"Here comes David to play for you, Father," said Jonathan on the other side of the table.

"Why is he coming?" Saul demanded in an angry burst.

"Remember you asked him to play his lyre for you."

"Oh no. Well. Go meet him and show him in."

David's fingers strummed across the strings with delicate precision. The resonating music filled the house. In spite of himself, Saul's tense mind began to relax. His troubled spirit felt the soft, vibrations of the finely-calibrated tune. His heart welled up in harmony with each titillating note. His eyelids lowered to shut out the morning light. Peace began to pervade his soul. But just then Negal, the demon, blasted into the aura of peace. "This is the guy whom you saw on your throne."

Oh no. Saul recoiled in his mind, this man will wow everyone away from me. He is too much. How can I compete with such charm? God is no longer with me. He is with him. Saul fled the room to rave out of earshot, "David! David, David. What a dangerous soul. Would to God, Goliath had killed you. I dare not let you live." Curses and vulgarities followed.

The abandonment to hate opened Saul's heart to the underworld.

* * *

Negal leaped in, taking possession. "Won't Satan be proud of me!" said Negal to himself. "I have charge of Saul's faculties and I can invite other imps to help me take control of the kingdom of Israel."

* * *

The resulting effect instantly demented Saul's thought processes. He grabbed his spear, crept stealthily to the doorway leading to the room he had just left. Then he lurched through the doorway and flung the sharp-headed instrument straight at the musician. But David saw it coming and leaped out of the trajectory. The spear rammed into the

Foresight

wall, vibrating with the intensity of the thrust.

Saul's intense jealousy of David continued to build until David had to hide from him. Saul suspected that eighty-five priests of the Town of Nob were plotting with David to overthrow him as king. So he killed them all in spite of their protests of innocence. After this, the Lord totally forsook Saul. Years later God allowed the Philistines to kill Saul and his sons in battle.

David became king. He set up his throne in Jerusalem and established his headquarters there. David ruled for forty years. He was the greatest king Israel ever had. Under his leadership Israel experienced the blessings and favor of God. They came out of the *despair* Saul had brought to them. The kingdom expanded through military conquest.

David loved God and faithfully lived out his rule as a man after God's own heart except for one serious breakdown. He faithfully prayed and sought the Lord and was filled with his joy. He lived in fellowship with God. His Psalms abounded with dramatic expressions of love for God and the joy of the Lord:

> O God, you are my God; earnestly I seek you;
>   my soul thirsts for you; my flesh faints for you,
>   as in a dry and weary land where there is no water.
> So I have looked upon you in the sanctuary,
> beholding your power and glory.
> Because your steadfast love is better than life,
>   my lips will praise you.
> So I will bless you as long as I live;
>   in your name I will lift up my hands.
> My soul will be satisfied as with fat and rich food,
> and my mouth will praise you with joyful lips,
> when I remember you upon my bed,
>   and meditate on you in the watches of the night;

> for you have been my help,
>   and in the shadow of your wings I will sing for joy.
> My soul clings to you;
>   your right hand upholds me" (Psalm 63:1-8).

David subdued the Philistines, the people of Goliath he had killed with his sling in his younger days. He conquered enemy nations—the Ammonites, the Moabites, the Syrians, and the Edomites. His conquests expanded the kingdom of Israel to include all the land God promised to Abraham. This included

> the land of the Kenites, the Kenizzites, the Kadmonites, [20] the Hittites, the Perizzites, the Rephaim, the Amorites, the Canaanites, the Girgashites and the Jebusites (Genesis 15:19-21).

Later this territory was described as

> all the kingdoms from the Euphrates to the land of the Philistines and to the border of Egypt (1 Kings 4:21).

Since David was of the *remnant* keeping the covenant, God reconfirmed the *covenant* with him and added to it:

> "I have made a covenant with my chosen one; I have sworn to David my servant:
> 'I will establish your offspring forever, and build your throne for all generations'" (Psalm 89:3-4).

Later the Lord would say through Jeremiah: "I will fulfill the good promise that I have spoken concerning the house of Israel and the house of Judah. In those days and at that time I will cause a Righteous Branch to sprout up for David, and he will administer justice and righteousness in the land. In those days Judah will be saved, and Jerusalem will dwell securely, and this is what she will be named: The Lord Is Our Righteousness" (Jeremiah 33:14-16).

Foresight

Chapter 15

Seventy Years

Daniel stood looking longingly in the direction of the land of Israel from where he had just come to Babylon. Here he was alone with his thoughts: I will not see my homeland for at least seventy years according to the prophet Jeremiah. I know the history of 500 years under human kings. We provoked God to turn us over to the captivity I now experience.

King Saul's reign began this period of the kings. The history saw a few good kings and some following the Lord for a period of time. Others simply worshiped idols and consumed the resources of the kingdom on themselves. David was the only one of the first three who wholeheartedly did what was right in the sight of the Lord. He did have some serious missteps but repented in deep sorrow when confronted with his sin.

Following Kings Saul, David, and Solomon, the kingdom divided. Rehoboam became king over the southern division—the kingdom of Judah composed of the tribes of Judah and Benjamin. Jeroboam became king over the northern division—the kingdom of Israel composed of the other ten tribes. A few of the kings of the

Foresight

kingdom of Israel made partial attempts to follow the Lord. But God didn't view any of the eighteen that reigned after the division as doing right in his sight. They kept provoking the Lord God to anger. Finally, by 722 B.C. God had had enough and brought in the Assyrian army to carry most of them captive to Assyria. The kingdom was no more.

Daniel's thoughts went to the kingdom of Judah. I know the kings of the kingdom of Judah did better. But there were twelve bad kings who reigned in wickedness, interspersed with eight good kings. The eight good kings, Josiah, Hezekiah, Jotham, Azariah. Amaziah, Joash, Jehoshaphat, and Asa destroyed idols and did what was right in the sight of the Lord. But the ever-persistent tendency of Judah to turn to idols finally prevailed.

In 605 B.C., God allowed the Chaldeans to burn Jerusalem and the temple. They carried captive most of Judah, my people, here. After he burned Jerusalem, the king of Babylon set up puppet kings who ruled for a short time.

I know the kings stood in the way of God's leadership to the people. Oh how the thought pains me! We Israelites brought this worldly rule of kings on ourselves by rejecting God as our king and demanding an earthly king in Samuel's day. We wanted to have a visible, physical presence to trust in that we could experience physically with our five senses. Our hearts were hard and not tuned to spiritually experiencing God who is Spirit.

The kings we trusted grew corrupt, consuming the kingdom resources on themselves as they turned the hearts of our people to idols. The idol worship was a further expression of our unspiritual preoccupation with the sensory and the material. Idol worship quickly became sensual involving male and female prostitutes. Yes, this focused our living on pleasuring our senses with sensuality instead of living in the joy of the Lord through pray, fellowship with the true God, and study of his word. But the idol worship didn't stop with the sexual immorality. It even led people to offer their children on the fire-heated, red-hot iron arms of Moloch. Parents watched their children burn, hoping their sacrifice would bring the financial prosperity that Moloch worship promised. No wonder God allowed the Chaldeans to plunder us and destroy our land as he had proclaimed he would do by the mouth of Jeremiah:

> "For the children of Israel and the children of Judah have done nothing but evil in my sight from their youth. The children of Israel

have done nothing but provoke me to anger by the work of their hands, declares the Lord.

This city has aroused my anger and wrath, from the day it was built to this day, so that I will remove it from my sight because of all the evil of the children of Israel and the children of Judah that they did to provoke me to anger—their kings and their officials, their priests and their prophets, the men of Judah and the inhabitants of Jerusalem.

They have turned to me their back and not their face. And though I have taught them persistently, they have not listened to receive instruction. ³They set up their abominations in the house that is called by my name, to defile it.

They built the high places of Baal in the Valley of the Son of Hinnom, to offer up their sons and daughters to Molech, though I did not command them, nor did it enter into my mind, that they should do this abomination, to cause Judah to sin (Jeremiah 32:30-35).

Foresight

Chapter 16

End of the Seventy Years

Daniel climbed the stairs to the elegant balcony on the rooftop of the ornamental house provided for him to live in. He stood at the rail and slowly turned a full 360 degrees surveying the horizon of the mighty kingdom. Since his captivity began, the Medes and Persians had conquered the Babylonians, and now Daniel served King Darius the Mede in the Medo-Persian Empire.

Daniel looked up to heaven in prayerful meditation: God's judgment against my nation brought me to Babylon. Being away from my beloved land has been the trial of my life. Here I only have the amount of freedom the king's whims allow. But God has used this bondage to give me great opportunities to introduce people to the Lord.

The first real break came when the kingdom was under the Chaldeans. When Nebuchadnezzar was king, he dreamed a dramatic dream. Then he demanded the magicians, mediums, and sorcerers tell him both what he had dreamed and the interpretation of the dream. Of course they weren't able to tell him what he had dreamed. So Nebuchadnezzar flew into a rage and issued a decree to destroy all the wise men in Babylon. They came for me because I was considered one of the wise men, I asked for some time to hear from God.

Foresight

God told me the dream and the interpretation. The dream involved several metaphors of truths that are keys to understanding God's kingdom and its quests. These metaphors will become symbols of the same key truths presented in future scripture. I stood before the king and relayed what God had revealed:

"You saw, O king, and behold, a great image. This image, mighty and of exceeding brightness, stood before you, and its appearance was frightening. The head of this image was of fine gold, its chest and arms of silver, its middle and thighs of bronze, its legs of iron, its feet partly of iron and partly of clay.

As you looked, a stone was cut out by no human hand, and it struck the image on its feet of iron and clay, and broke them in pieces. Then the iron, the clay, the bronze, the silver, and the gold, all together were broken in pieces, and became like the chaff of the summer threshing floors; and the wind carried them away, so that not a trace of them could be found. But the stone that struck the image became a great mountain and filled the whole earth.

"This was the dream. Now we will tell the king its interpretation. You, O king, the king of kings, to whom the God of heaven has given the kingdom, the power, and the might, and the glory, and into whose hand he has given, wherever they dwell, the children of man, the beasts of the field, and the birds of the heavens, making you rule over them all—you are the head of gold.

Another kingdom inferior to you shall arise after you, and yet a third kingdom of bronze, which shall rule over all the earth. And there shall be a fourth kingdom, strong as iron, because iron breaks to pieces and shatters all things. And like iron that crushes, it shall break and crush all these. And as you saw the feet and toes, partly of potter's clay and partly of iron, it shall be a divided kingdom, but some of the firmness of iron shall be in it, just as you saw iron mixed with the soft clay. And as the toes of the feet were partly iron and partly clay, so the kingdom shall be partly strong and partly brittle. As you saw the iron mixed with soft clay, so they will mix with one another in marriage, but they will not hold together, just as iron does not mix with clay.

And in the days of those kings the God of heaven will set up a kingdom that shall never be destroyed, nor shall the kingdom be left to another people. It shall break in pieces all these kingdoms and bring them to an end, and it shall stand forever, just as you saw that a stone was cut from a mountain by no human hand, and that it broke in pieces the iron, the bronze, the clay, the silver, and the gold. A great God has made known to the king what shall be after this. The dream is certain, and its interpretation sure" (Daniel 2:31-45).

As Daniel continued to reflect, he remembered: The king was overjoyed and praised God for the revelation. He made me ruler of all the province of Babylon and the head of the wise men.

The golden head was Nebuchadnezzar's Babylonian kingdom. The silver chest and arms turned out to be the Medo-Persian kingdom which is now in power. The brass belly and thigh will be a Grecian Empire yet to come. Only the future will tell what kingdom the iron legs turns out to be.

Nebuchadnezzar loved my interpretation because it exalted him as greater than the three kingdoms to follow. But the main significance of the dream was "the stone cut from a mountain not by human hand"[15] It was destined to crush all the earthly kingdoms for attempting to rule apart from God and hijacking the worship due the Almighty. God's stone-kingdom will bring them to an end but will itself endure forever.

Daniel's spiritual discernment was in full alert as he continued to ponder: The stone-cut-from-a-mountain kingdom will be the spiritual kingdom of God. Our earthly kingdom—born out of demanding a king to make us like the other nations—miserably failed. But even now, God's stone-cut-from-a-mountain—consisting of all the forces of heaven—is expanding its power on the earth. Actually, it was the power that enabled the Medes and the Persians to conquer Babylon. And it is coming to bear on all the political forces of this world. God is sending forth his angels to keep his agenda on track.

---

[15] Daniel 2:45

Foresight

Daniel stroked his beard with his right hand as he remembered a dream he had after Nebuchadnezzar's dream (Daniel 7): My dream showed animals representing the same four kingdoms of the king's dream: a lion represented the gold head of Nebuchadnezzar's Babylonian kingdom. A bear represented the silver, Medo-Persian Empire. A leopard represented the brass, Grecian kingdom yet to come. Another terrifying and dreadful and exceedingly strong beast with large iron teeth represented the iron legs kingdom. Its identity, not yet revealed, was shown to follow the Grecian kingdom. And in connection with the iron leg kingdom, an arrogant Little Horn arose to do much havoc.

Oh yes, and I dreamed another dream. In that dream the same Little Horn came from the brass, Grecian Kingdom instead of the iron kingdom. Evidently, he will rise amid both of them. But in my first dream a son of man defeated the Little Horn. This son of man, the coming Messiah

> was given dominion
>   and glory and a kingdom,
> that all peoples, nations, and languages
>   should serve him;
> his dominion is an everlasting dominion,
>   which shall not pass away,
> and his kingdom one
>   that shall not be destroyed (Daniel 7:14).

Daniel drew a deep breath in full awareness of the spiritual revelation he was gaining: The coming son of man will be the king of the stone-cut-from-a-mountain kingdom. His kingdom will conquer the earthly kingdoms. This understanding is intended to inspire a remnant of us of Abraham's seed. We are to be ready to return to the Promised Land to give birth to the Messiah according to Isaiah's prophecy:

> For to us a child is born,
>   to us a son is given;
> and the government shall be upon his shoulder,
>   and his name shall be called
> Wonderful Counselor, Mighty God,
>   Everlasting Father, Prince of Peace.

End of the Seventy Years

> Of the increase of his government and of peace
> there will be no end,
> on the throne of David and over his kingdom,
> to establish it and to uphold it
> with justice and with righteousness
> from this time forth and forevermore.
> The zeal of the Lord of hosts will do this (Isaiah 9:6-7).

Daniel stroked his snow-white beard with more memories: The Medo-Persian kingdom in my dream has come and conquered the Babylonian Empire. Under King Darius, I was thrown into the den of lions for being true to my God. But of course the Lord shut the lion's mouths and they did not hurt me. Praise be to God. I continue to minister in the Medo-Persian Empire.

Foresight

Chapter 17

Seventy Weeks of Years

Daniel turned his attention to what Jeremiah had prophesied concerning the seventy-year captivity in Babylon of which he was a part. From this he realized the captivity was about to end. God had great things in store for those who were about to be set free.

> For thus says the Lord: When seventy years are completed for Babylon, I will visit you, and I will fulfill to you my promise and bring you back to this place. For I know the plans I have for you, declares the Lord, plans for welfare and not for evil, to give you a future and a hope.
>
> Then you will call upon me and come and pray to me, and I will hear you. You will seek me and find me, when you seek me with all your heart. I will be found by you, declares the Lord, and I will restore your fortunes and gather you from all the nations and all the places where I have driven you, declares the Lord, and I will bring you back to the place from which I sent you into exile (Jeremiah 29:10-14).

What a challenge to pray, thought Daniel: The seventy years are up.

Foresight

God's plans for his people's "wellbeing, not for disaster," to give them "a future and a hope" are on the horizon. My heart is bursting with urgency to seek God. I have confessed my sins and the sins of my people. Nothing dare stand in the way of receiving this very bright future God has promised us, his beloved people. But I don't just want goodies from God.

I want intimate empathy with my Lord. I want to know and embrace the heart of God. I have always been in touch with the Almighty—close enough to have interpretations of the king's dreams revealed to me. I received much understanding of future earthly kingdoms to come. But now I seek an even greater intimacy of understanding. I must have a sense of direction to offer those who look to me for God's leadership.

* * *

"Gabriel, I have exciting news," declared Michael. "Some intel from God's Book of Truth[16] has just been released to a slightly lower level of security classification. This intelligence is to be released to those highly treasured of God. It will reveal basic truths and longer-range plans of God to Daniel.

"How fascinating! But this means some of the intel of the Book of Truth will now be verbalized in human language. Daniel will certainly reveal the intelligence to his people by tongue and pen. Satan will be able to listen in and observe every word."

"Oh yes. You are right. But don't worry. It will come in coded language that only those with a high level of spiritual discernment will understand. Even Daniel will not be able to interpret everything, especially what pertains to the more distant future. Some of the intel will be left for future highly-treasured ones to discern from Daniel's writings. The time for some of the intelligence to play out is here. It is here *"already but not yet"* in its full form. Daniel will have understanding of all that requires action on his part.

---

[16] Daniel 10:21

"Furthermore, the intel is designed to manipulate Satan into actually advancing God's cause. As clever as Satan is, he will only understand enough to respond in the way God wants him to. The intel will serve as counterintelligence to trigger his rage into a reckless attack. He will plan evil but end up delivering what God plans for good."

"Like selling Joseph into Egypt," laughed Gabriel.

"Yes indeed. We angels are still laughing our holy heads off over that one. The devil is so evil he cannot comprehend the process of bringing about good. This is his downfall. It is really laughable to know that his whole campaign against God is serving God's purpose: It offers people the choice to go against God so they can choose the opposite which is to obey God. You're getting into deep stuff there, Michael."

"Yes. Yes! Let's get back to business. Are you ready to reveal the new intelligence from the Book of Truth[17] to Daniel?"

"Indeed. I am ready."

* * *

Daniel prayed in great agony:

> O my God, incline your ear and hear. Open your eyes and see our desolations, and the city that is called by your name. For we do not present our pleas before you because of our righteousness, but because of your great mercy. O Lord, hear; O Lord, forgive. O Lord, pay attention and act. Delay not, for your own sake, O my God, because your city and your people are called by your name" (Daniel 9:18-19).

"Daniel, your prayer has been heard," interrupted Gabriel:

---

[17] Daniel 10:2

Foresight

> "I have now come out to give you insight and understanding. At the beginning of your pleas for mercy a word went out, and I have come to tell it to you, for you are greatly loved. Therefore consider the word and understand the vision.
>
> "Seventy weeks are decreed about your people and your holy city, to finish the transgression, to put an end to sin, and to atone for iniquity, to bring in everlasting righteousness, to seal both vision and prophet, and to anoint a most holy place (Daniel 9:22-24).

Gabriel's response to Daniel's prayer has referenced seventy weeks. These seventy weeks are actually seventy weeks of year-long days, adding up to 490 years. This shows an important key to understanding prophecy. One application of the prophecy may refer to literal twenty-four-hour days. Another application may refer to year-long days. Seventy weeks, taken literally, are 490 days. But since the days are year-long days in this case, the time span is 490 years. And within the 490 years are three time-spans.

As Gabriel continues the explanation, Daniel sees that the first time-span of forty-nine years (seven weeks) will see the temple rebuilt. The second one of 434 years (sixty-two weeks) will be a space of time leading up to the third time-span. The third time-span of seven years (one week) will bring the Anointed One. He "will make a firm *covenant*" for seven years and "put a stop to sacrifice and offering" in the middle of the seven years. Later, a prince will come to "destroy the city and the sanctuary."

Suddenly, Gabriel was gone. The potent message boggled Daniel's mind.

"I will not be alive to see all of this," Daniel spoke aloud, "but the future is bright. Who will this Anointed One be? Well it surely must be the child Isaiah prophesied about:

> For to us a child is born,
>   to us a son is given;
>   and the government shall be upon his shoulder,

> and his name shall be called
> Wonderful Counselor, Mighty God,
> Everlasting Father, Prince of Peace.
> Of the increase of his government and of peace
>   there will be no end,
> on the throne of David and over his kingdom,
>   to establish it and to uphold it
> with justice and with righteousness
>   from this time forth and forevermore.
> The zeal of the Lord of hosts will do this (Isaiah 9:6-7).

Daniel's eyes widened suddenly: I now see this prophecy in greater depth than ever before. The child whom all my people recognize to be the Messiah will actually be "Mighty God." No wonder his "dominion" will be vast and his "prosperity" will never end. God himself will be King Messiah of this "kingdom." I know that none of my contemporary scribes grasp this. They are looking for another mere earthly king, one as good as King David, but not God himself. Somehow this Anointed One will be at once God and man.

This is mind-boggling. The coming son-of-man-messiah, the Anointed One, will also be God. Does this mean he actually will be the Son of God, of the same essence as the Father?

Come to think of it, Isaiah has prophesied something else about Messiah that might correlate with this:

> Surely he has borne our griefs
>   and carried our sorrows;
> yet we esteemed him stricken,
>   smitten by God, and afflicted.
> But he was pierced for our transgressions;
>   he was crushed for our iniquities;
> upon him was the chastisement that brought us peace,
>   and with his wounds we are healed.
> All we like sheep have gone astray;
>   we have turned—every one—to his own way;

Foresight

> and the Lord has laid on him
> the iniquity of us all (Isaiah 53:4-6).

Things were coming together in Daniel's mind. Isaiah says, "The Lord has laid on him the iniquity of us all." This one who will bear "the iniquity of us all" must be the Anointed One who "will make a firm covenant" for seven years (the seventieth week) and then put a "put a stop to sacrifice and offering" in the middle of the seven years. A shiver went up Daniel's spine: Evidently, this Anointed One is going to be "pierced because of our rebellion, crushed because of our iniquities" and take the "punishment for our peace" in the middle of this week. And this will "put a stop to sacrifice and offering" because no more animal sacrifices will be needed.

I have realized that animal sacrifices can only be token sacrifices, for sin is much more serious than the death of a lamb or goat. Is the Anointed One going to be the ultimate atonement, the ultimate sacrifice and offering for sin to redeem all the token sacrifices?

This could be true but why would God allow a prince to "destroy the city and the sanctuary" after he inspires people to rebuild it? Another shiver of understanding went up Daniel's spine: Obviously, there will be no need for a temple if no more animal sacrifices are needed.

Daniel stroked his hair back across his head with his left hand: I will not live to see how all the details will play out. But what a joy. God has not forgotten his people. He is planning a bright future filled with hope for those who will seek him.

* * *

"I wish I could reveal more of the Book of Truth to Daniel," sighed Michael. "Even now God is preparing Cyrus the Persian to become king in the place of Darius the Mede. And he will issue the decree to "restore and rebuild Jerusalem." A rebuilt temple will be finished at the end of the first seven weeks (forty-nine years) in spite of a lot of hindrances. The next sixty-two weeks (434 years) will bring the world to the last week, seven years of the ministry of the 'Anointed One.'"

Seventy Weeks of Years

"Gabriel, you must go and give him more intel on the Little Horn he saw in his dreams because he will be a king who will greatly impact Israel. Daniel will not be able to understand all of it. But he will write the intel down to give foresight to those who will need it at the time of its fulfillment."

* * *

Gabriel told Daniel of a king of the North and a king of the South who will be at war with each other. Eventually, the king of the north will fall, be assassinated and then:

> "A contemptible person to whom royal majesty has not been given. He shall come in without warning and obtain the kingdom by flatteries....
>
> "He shall...be enraged and take action against the holy covenant. He shall turn back and pay attention to those who forsake the holy covenant. Forces from him shall appear and profane the temple and fortress, and shall take away the regular burnt offering. And they shall set up the abomination that makes desolate. He shall seduce with flattery those who violate the covenant, but the people who know their God shall stand firm and take action....
>
> "He shall exalt himself and magnify himself above every god, and shall speak astonishing things against the God of gods. He shall prosper till the indignation is accomplished; for what is decreed shall be done....
>
> Yet he shall come to his end, with none to help him. (excerpts from Daniel 11:21-45).

As the revelation poured forth, Daniel's eyes widened: This is the Little Horn. I saw him in my two dreams of rising kingdoms, but now I know this "despised" one will not just create havoc to other earthly kingdoms. "He will rage against the holy covenant" and "desecrate the temple" with some kind of abomination. "But the people who know their God will be strong and

Foresight

take action." Yes, God will always have a remnant to live out his covenant and reap the promise: "I will bless those who bless you, I will curse anyone who treats you with contempt, and all the peoples on earth will be blessed through you" (Genesis 12:3).

Chapter 18

Zechariah's Visions

"Gabriel. I have important direction from God Almighty. The prophet Zechariah has been cleared to receive intel from the Book of Truth directly. Zechariah like Daniel has qualified as one highly favored of God."

"All right, Michael. I will unlock the Book of Truth with the key: *the kingdom of God conquers the kingdom of this world*, then we will channel the truth from the book to Zechariah in the form of visions.

"Darius the Persian had succeeded Cyrus as the king of the Empire. Obviously, he was not Darius the Mede who ruled as king directly after the Medo-Persian forces conquered Babylon. Zechariah will see visions with from the Book of Truth with our help, and you, Gabriel, will need to be present to answer the questions he will have about the visions. As in Daniel's visions, these visions will present metaphors of truths that are keys to understanding God's kingdom and its quests. These metaphors will become symbols of the same key truths presented in future scripture."

Foresight

* * *

Zechariah was back in the land of Israel after the seventy-year captivity. Here he enjoyed his prayer time, study of God's word, and fellowship with his maker more than ever before. The leather-skinned, white-haired prophet rested on his bed. He and the people he ministered to needed some encouragement. The land was in ruins. The temple had been destroyed by the Babylonians and the wall around Jerusalem was largely broken down. Suddenly a vision engulfed him.

A man appeared, riding on a *chestnut horse.* He stood among the myrtle trees in the valley. Behind him were *chestnut, brown,* and white horses. Zechariah asked, "What are these, my lord?"

An angel replied:

> "I will show you what they are." So the man who was standing among the myrtle trees answered, "These are they whom the Lord has sent to patrol the earth" (Zechariah 1:10).

* * *

Looking on Michael clasped his hands together with a firm grip as he explained, "Yes, God allows people to make choices to do evil, but he does not allow those choices to wreck his agenda. God has designed his creation to function according to certain natural laws. But his horses of providence must intervene in the course of history to keep his agenda on track for the kingdom of God to conquer the kingdom of Satan. This vision shows them ready to go forth to patrol the earth the moment God calls for them to act.

* * *

An angel now addressed the Lord on Zechariah's behalf:

Zechariah's Visions

"O Lord of hosts, how long will you have no mercy on Jerusalem and the cities of Judah, against which you have been angry these seventy years?" (Zechariah (1:12).

The answer came immediately for Zechariah to hear:

"Cry out, Thus says the Lord of hosts: I am exceedingly jealous for Jerusalem and for Zion. And I am exceedingly angry with the nations that are at ease; for while I was angry but a little, they furthered the disaster. Therefore, thus says the Lord, I have returned to Jerusalem with mercy; my house shall be built in it, declares the Lord of hosts, and the measuring line shall be stretched out over Jerusalem.

"Cry out again, Thus says the Lord of hosts: My cities shall again overflow with prosperity, and the Lord will again comfort Zion and again choose Jerusalem" (Zechariah 1:14-17).

Zechariah did a mental assessment. Yes, God is about to turn his horses loose to change the course of events. Theses horses of providential intervention, controlled by God's Spirit, are about to disrupt the calm and quiet of the natural development of history to revive his people to a strong relationship with him. He is measuring out the blessings he will give in a future Jerusalem with a focus on its Zion characteristic. The term Zion has always had a lofty, spiritual connotation. In this vision I am seeing, Jerusalem and Zion must be metaphors of something greater than an earthly city.

As Zechariah meditated on this, the angel projected another vision from the Book of Truth to Zechariah with these words:

"Jerusalem shall be inhabited as villages without walls, because of the multitude of people and livestock in it. And I will be to her a wall of fire all around, declares the Lord, and I will be the glory in her midst" (Zechariah (2:4).

With great enthusiasm, the angel continued:

Sing and rejoice, O daughter of Zion, for behold, I come and I will dwell in your midst, declares the Lord. And many nations shall join themselves to the Lord in that day, and shall be my people. And I will dwell in your midst, and you shall know that the Lord of hosts has

Foresight

> sent me to you. And the Lord will inherit Judah as his portion in the holy land, and will again choose Jerusalem" (Zechariah 2:10-13).

* * *

Hovering close by, Michael realized that the interpretation of these visions would gradually come to the Zechariah and others. But Michael's eyes glowed with interpretive understanding of this intel: The horses of providence of the stone-cut-from-a-mountain will inaugurate a series of events to bring a conqueror who will come to be known as Alexander the Great. This conqueror will establish the third empire. This will be the third kingdom, the brass belly and thigh of Nebuchadnezzar's dream. It will also be the one-horned goat of Daniel's dream-prophecy. And it will disrupt the calm and quiet with his charging conquest. He will conquer almost all of the kingdoms of the world of this time. The present empire of Persia will fall before him as well as the other kingdoms.

However, Alexander the Great will not disturb the Jews. In fact, when the high priest will request that they might continue in the ways of their forefathers, Alexander will grant all they desire.[18] And since the king of the far-reaching empire will have this attitude toward Israel, Israel will be protected during his reign and he will have a certain amount of God's favor.

Yes, Michael reflected: the foundation of the temple has already been laid under Zerubbabel's leadership. And the rebuilding will be finished. God's people will flood back into Jerusalem from the lands of their captivity. The walls will be built around her under a man named Nehemiah.

Therefore, the prophecy of a Jerusalem inhabited without walls" will be a different Jerusalem of another future development. The Jerusalem "without walls" will be built in the distant future. But it will be foreshadowed in the earthly Jerusalem that is about to be restored and have walls. The city without walls will not be earthly. It will be a spiritual city for all people.

* * *

---

[18] Antiquities of the Jews, Josephus 11.338

Zechariah's Visions

The angel showed Zechariah another vision in which Joshua the high priest stood before another angel. This other angel said to Joshua:

> "Hear now, O Joshua the high priest, you and your friends who sit before you, for they are men who are a sign: behold, I will bring my servant the Branch. For behold, on the stone that I have set before Joshua, on a single stone with seven eyes I will engrave its inscription, declares the Lord of hosts, and I will remove the iniquity of this land in a single day" (Zechariah 3:8-9).

* * *

Gabriel shaded his eyes with his right hand and gazed through the spirit world. His brow was furrowed with wrinkles as he thought, Zechariah has written down all of this intelligence about the Branch to come. Again, as before about similar intel, he was concerned that it could be read by the demons. The Branch picture portrays the Messiah who will be a pure and holy high priest. Why would God allow this new intel to be known to the demons?

Michael read the concern on Gabriel's countenance. "Don't worry, Gabriel. Remember the interpretive understanding you are getting will not be known to Satan. Like we have observed in the past, I suspect this intelligence will only serve as more counterintelligence to Satan. It will provoke him to do the evil that God intends for good. When Satan sees this intel, he will be enraged with a single-minded focus. He literally will have a hell-bent determination to destroy the Messiah. This focus will make him totally blind to the consequences for his kingdom."

* * *

Foresight

Zechariah fell asleep from the mental strain of trying to comprehend the meaning of these visions.

After some time, an angel woke him up to ask him, "What do you see?"

Zechariah replied:

> "I see, and behold, a lampstand all of gold, with a bowl on the top of it, and seven lamps on it, with seven lips on each of the lamps that are on the top of it. And there are two olive trees by it, one on the right of the bowl and the other on its left" (Zechariah 4:2-3).

Zechariah asked, "What are these?"

The angel answered:

> "These are the two anointed ones who stand by the Lord of the whole earth" (Zechariah 4:14).

By this answer, Zechariah understood what the picture was about and said to himself, "The one olive tree gives light through the lampstand from the word of God. The other olive tree gives light through the lampstand from the fulfillment of the Word. The word of God is the commandment to build the temple and the fulfillment of the Word is the temple being built."

"The one 'anointed one' is the communicated word of God. The other 'anointed one' is the testimony of it being fulfilled," Zechariah said to himself. "These two witnesses must be extremely important to God to be portrayed in this elaborate way as standing before the Lord of the whole earth. Evidently these two are going to play an important part in God's cause going forward.

The angels brought another vision. Three women appeared. Two had wings carrying the third in a basket. They flew to Shinar to build a shrine. Shinar, another name for Babylon, was a place of *humanistic religion,* the product established in old Babel.

* * *

Zechariah's Visions

The two flying women could be interpreted as sensualism and materialism carrying the false faith of humanism to build a shrine to that faith, thought Gabriel.

From the Book of Truth, Michael saw into the future. He saw the three -isms manifesting themselves in the Greek culture in Alexander the Great's conquest of the Persian Empire. He saw women becoming sacred temple prostitutes of the Zeus worship developed in Greece.

The Greeks will seek to unite all the kingdoms of the world in the sensuous worship of Zeus and his hierarchy of gods. *Sensualism* will advance the lust-of-the-eyes *materialism* with a focus on the material human body. The false, *humanistic* faith involved will promote kinky, gross sexual perversions as righteous worship of Zeus. Yes, the Zeus worship will drive these -isms of the devil. But even after Zeus worship will become outdated, *sensualism, materialism* and *humanism* will live on. These -isms, developed in the Garden of Eden, will continue to influence people to turn from God and his ways.

* * *

Zechariah now had his head in his hands in serious contemplation as the angels began to unfold another vision. In this vision the horses appeared again, only this time they pulled chariots. Evidently this means their work was more impactful, he thought. "What of these?" asked Zechariah.

"These are going out to the four winds of heaven, after presenting themselves before the Lord of all the earth. The chariot with the *black horses* goes toward the north country, the *white ones* go after them, and the *dappled ones* go toward the south country." When the strong horses came out, they were impatient to go and patrol the earth. And he said, "Go, patrol the

Foresight

> earth." So they patrolled the earth. Then he cried to me, "Behold, those who go toward the north country have set my Spirit at rest in the north country" (Zechariah 6:5-8).

Zechariah stared off into the distance. This much he understood: the Lord of hosts was sending out his horses of providence to change the course of history even in his time. God's horses were going forth to *patrol* the earth to keep God's overall agenda on track for conquering the kingdom of this world. This was preparing the way for the Lord's stone-cut-from-a-mountain (his kingdom) to fill the whole earth.

Chapter 19

The Little Horn

"I, the great manipulator of human destiny, have called you, my adoring demons, to this meeting to discuss new strategies. The Sumer worship has long since lost its luster because you, An, have not continued to promote its worship."

"You hateful egotist. How dare you blame me? You preempted Sumer worship with your stupid demons, Baal, Ashteroth, and Moloch."

"Stupid? You're nuts. I ruined both the Kingdom of Israel and the Kingdom of Judah with the worship of our demons posing as gods of rain, wind, lightning, and earth fertility."

"Oh yah? Why do we now have the Kingdom of Israel back in their land with a rebuilt temple and City of Jerusalem? Why are the Jews faithfully offering sacrifices to God and keeping the annual feasts designed to keep them in touch with their Maker? The *covenant* people of God are far more conscious of what he desires and much more committed to him. You actually played right into God's hands. Baal, Ashtaroth, and Moloch could only entice the rebellious ones away from God. Now God has a purified *remnant* determined to be true to him."

Foresight

"Shut your ugly mouth right now, An," boomed Satan.

"Put him in chains," cried Baal.

"Yes. And then give the little devil a sound beating," shouted Ashteroth.

"Oh, the truth hurts. Doesn't it?" smirked An.

"Now that does it!" declared Moloch. "We can have no talk of truth. We only operate in falsehood."

"Take him away and do with him as you wish," snarled Satan.

Several demons pounced on An and dragged him away with An cursing all the way in his deep guttural voice until they were out of earshot. Heads hung in forced acknowledgment of hated truth. Dread filled the atmosphere. Deep down every imp knew they were fighting a losing battle, but their only hope of getting their minds off this reality was to fight on.

"Okay. You dismal beings, you will not help yourselves by thinking of failure," said Satan. "As I was saying, I have a brilliant plan to test those whom An thinks are so committed to God. I'll bet the Israelites are still prone to worship something they can see and handle—something appealing to their senses more than their spirits. Our perversion of godly love, namely the *lust-of-the-flesh sensualism*, obsesses people with gratifying their senses with pleasure. This diverts them from spiritual worship of God and developing their spirits for doing so. Furthermore, our perversion of God-given *hope*, namely the *lust-of-the-eyes materialism*, is certainly our root of evil. It keeps people from being heavenly minded. And our perversion of *faith*, namely *pride-of-life humanism*, keeps people pridefully dependent on themselves apart from God. Our -isms cause people to live just to pleasure their senses instead of finding the joy of the Lord through prayer, study of God's word, and fellowship with their Maker.

"Our strategy against God will always involve our three -isms. What people want they tend to believe in. Their *sensualistic* and

The Little Horn

materialistic lusts drive them to the faith of *humanism*—to believe in the gods that gratify these lusts."

"Well, what is your new strategy, Egotistic Lord?" asked Zeus.

"Oh, I was waiting for this question. I knew that the one who would ask would be acknowledging my cunning and be the rightful one to head the new worship."

"At your service, my Lord Evil One."

"Very good. You are to head up a classy form of worship—a kind to which Baal, Ashteroth, and Moloch could not rise. There will be no more sacrificing of children. That is certain to offend the more civilized society of today. Your worship will appeal to those who see themselves as having refined sensitivities."

"But still appeal to the senses more than to the spirit," inserted Zeus.

"Exactly. I knew you would be the one to head this new religion," declared Satan.

"Actually, I have been planning to present this kind of religion to you for some time, knowing you would be able to discern whether it was a good idea or not," replied Zeus.

"Glad you said that. Don't ever get the idea you can surpass my intelligence. So what are your thoughts?"

"Well, we are going to need a lot of help. I have already enlisted my team of demons. They are eager to get started."

"You did this without consulting me first? How dare you?"

"Oh, most brilliant strategist of human manipulation, please don't be offended. I wanted to have everything in readiness, so you would not have to spend your time doing the research, seeing you are fully occupied with leading our great debaucherous, corrupting kingdom."

"Well, all right. Proceed," pronounced Satan.

"This is the team and their duties I propose to you, being ready to change anything you suggest.

"Artemis, you will be the goddess huntress and protectress of the

Foresight

living world.

"Dionysus, you will be the god of intoxication and sex.

"Aphrodite, you will be the goddess of love, sex, and beauty.

"Ares, you will be the god of bloodlust.

"Hermes, you will be the god of fertility, music, luck, and deception.

"Eros, you will be god of sensual love, obsessive love of pleasure.

"Aphroditus, you will be god of male and female unity and the moon.

"Pan, you will be the god of fear and fields, groves, and wooded glens to promote sensuality.

"Gaia, you will be Earth Mother and goddess of the fertile earth."

"Wow," Satan spoke. "I am now more certain than ever that you are the one to head this new religious worship. You left no stone unturned to promote *sensualism*. I am ready to accept all as you propose. All of you devils, who have been named, arise and stand in line to receive your credentials for being gods. Then immediately present yourselves to Zeus for your first assignment."

* * *

Antiochus IV, the Syrian hostage in Rome, gazed at his likeness in the silver mirror.[19] Brushing his bushy locks back with both his hands from his face, he charmed himself. How much I look like Alexander the Great's handsome image on the Grecian coins. Surely, looking like the great conqueror will help me continue my campaign of flattery to seize control of the Grecian, Seleucid kingdom.

---

[19] The account of Antiochus IV and the rebellion against him presented through the rest of this chapter contains some imaginary descriptions of personalities and other minor details that seem to fit the narrative, but most of the account is taken from credible history.

The Little Horn

Antiochus reflected on the history of the domain. Alexander conquered the Medo-Persian Empire and greatly expanded it. When he died, the empire was divided to Alexander's generals. Seleucus took control of Babylon and expanded his Seleucid kingdom until it was the largest of the successor kingdoms of Alexanders Empire. His successor Seleucus II attempted to invade Egypt but was driven back by the Egyptian king. Following this the king of Egypt (the king of the South of Daniel's vision)[20] and the Seleucid King (the king of the North of Daniel's vision)[21] fought for control of the former Greek Empire through the years. The fourth king of the north, Antiochus III, expanded the Seleucid kingdom until it included almost all of Alexander's former empire.

Antiochus IV's face grimaced in pain as he recalled his father's setbacks. Antiochus III's army had fought its way into control of Asia Minor and parts of Europe. The Greeks were elated and surnamed Antiochus III "The Great" in memory of Alexander the Great. This allowed him to dub himself Antiochus the Great.

Antiochus reflected: The nasty Romans, after repeatedly warning my father to stay out of Asia Minor and Europe, defeated him at Thermopylae. A year later the Romans crushed him in the Battle of Magnesia. The resultant Treaty of Apamea required him to give up all of his gains in Asia Minor and Europe. He also had to pay yearly installments to pay back Rome for what his war cost them. He even had to surrender his war elephants and fleet of ships. The Romans also demanded 20 men including me as hostages. This is why I am in Rome.

"Ah, but this is not the end of the story," said Antiochus IV to his likeness in the mirror. "I have charmed the Romans into thinking I will turn the Seleucid Empire over to them if they release me. They have agreed to demand that my nephew, Demetrius, the current heir to the Seleucid, be hostage in my place. I conned them into doing this. Of course, my brother Seleucus IV, Demetrius's father, will have to

---

[20] Daniel 11:5-9
[21] Daniel 11:5-9

Foresight

be removed from the throne. He has been king since my father died. But Zeus will be glad to arrange this.

"After all, have I not committed myself to Zeus and his sensuous worship? Of course I was thrilled to do this because Zeus inspires me to continue my erotic pursuits. He helps me justify having sexual relations with many different people. The sacred prostitution in the Temple of Zeus gives me many opportunities. Neither the males nor the females can resist my gregarious, sensory charm and my effervescent personality.

"I have learned to flatter my way into the good graces of anyone I choose. And of course everyone will be inclined to look at me as the rightful heir to the kingdom when they see how much I look like the exceedingly handsome Alexander the Great. It will be very helpful to have Demetrius held hostage here in Rome."

~

The envoy from Rome drew a circle around King Antiochus IV. "You will answer me before you step out of this circle in the sand or take on the full force of the Roman military. Are you going to leave now and stop your invasion to take over Egypt?"

Antiochus glared with clenched teeth, and lips drawn back tight. Since he had become king through flattery and force, he had been expanding the Seleucid Empire through his military strength. He had Hellenized the various cultures of the domain into Zeus worship. This removed the divisiveness of various competing religions. It made all nations one people except some of the Israelites who worshiped the God of heaven.

Antiochus' brain spoke torments to him: Zeus should be happy with me. Why is my Greek god letting me down? Here I stand between my men and the Roman delegation with all eyes viewing my humiliation. Everyone knows I cannot take on Rome.

The envoy stood smirking with glee. "I can stand as long as you

The Little Horn

want, great king of Syria and worshiper of Zeus."

With redness now creeping up his neck and filling his tense face, Antiochus muttered, "I will leave." With that, he drove his chariot and horses away with the fury of a Jehu, leaving his large army struggling to catch up.

He obsessed over the thought: What can I do now to vent my wrath and restore my image? I have to do something drastic! After I have minted my likeness on the Seleucid coins with the inscription, Antiochus Epiphanes, meaning God manifest, the very incarnation of Zeus himself, I cannot remain humiliated. I have to put some people down. I must smash them to restore my image.

Before Antiochus and his army got out of Egypt in their return to Syria, a lone man came galloping on his horse from the north. Obviously, he was a messenger. He drew back on the reins as he rode up to the company. "I need to speak to my lord the King. I have news."

"Speak up, young man," said Antiochus as he rapidly approached the messenger.

"There has been a great rebellion in Jerusalem. Jason has driven Menelaus your appointed high priest from the temple."

"What? You mean to tell me Jason has rallied a great enough force of people to drive Menelaus from the priesthood? He has done this so he can be priest again?"

"Yes indeed, your Highest, Lord Zeus, God Manifest."

This was the object on which Antiochus needed to vent his wrath. He immediately sent his soldiers ahead to the land of Israel. "Cut everyone down you meet in Jerusalem," he bellowed.

In three days, 40,000–including women and children—lay dead on the ground and another 40,000 were being corralled to sell into slavery.

> Then Antiochus IV, sent letters by messengers unto Jerusalem and the cities of Judah that they should follow the strange laws of the land, And forbid burnt offerings,

Foresight

> and sacrifice, and drink offerings, in the temple; and that they should profane the sabbaths and festival days, And pollute the sanctuary and holy people, Set up altars, and groves, and chapels of idols, and sacrifice swine's flesh, and unclean beasts, That they should also leave their children uncircumcised, and make their souls abominable with all manner of uncleanness and profanation, To the end they might forget the law, and change all the ordinances. And whosoever would not do according to the commandment of the king, he said, he should die.[22]

Antiochus Epiphanes set up a statue of himself named Zeus in the temple and commanded everyone to worship the idol. He also instituted sacred prostitution and the other rites of Zeus worship.

But Antiochus Epiphanes would not be ready for the *stone-cut-from-a-mountain* which was now rolling his way. He was destined to encounter the judgment of this Almighty force.

The king sent his general to Modin, a rural town west of Jerusalem. Mattathias, the gray-headed local chief priest stood with his sword strapped to his side. Deep creases lined his forehead above piercing eyes. "What brings you here, sir?"

"The king has commanded you to sacrifice to Zeus to set an example to others because you are a leader here. Your nation should be like the other nations. All are worshiping Zeus. The king will honor you and your children with gifts of gold and silver."

"Are you out of your mind? Though all nations obey the king, my sons and I will not abandon the God of our fathers."

An apostate Jew came forward. "I will obey the king's command and offer the sacrifice." Mattathias' sword sliced through the air. The Jew jumped back, but not far enough. Blood gushed from his half-severed neck as he fell to the ground. Mattathias' sons charged the general and cut him down also.

---

[22] I Maccabees 1:44-50

The Little Horn

~

Judah Maccabeus hid in the trees with his ragtag guerrilla warriors that had formed under his father Mattathias' leadership. They watched General Apollonius approaching with an army that greatly outnumbered them. Antiochus Epiphanes had sent him.

Judah sent the word out to his warriors, "Be ready to fight for your God, your families, and your land. Be strong and courageous. God is with us and will give us the victory."

As the enemy drew abreast, Judah charged from his cover with the rest of the guerrillas. They surrounded the general's army before they could gather their wits. The Israelite guerrillas killed hundreds of them. Before the Samaritan forces could break out and flee, Judah killed Apollonius and took his sword.

Seron, the general of the army of Celesyria, heard the news and declared, "How dare these Jews be allowed to wreak such havoc in the Grecian empire and so greatly insult King Antiochus? I will put a stop to this in short order."

He gathered a much larger army than Apollonius had mustered and came against the guerrillas. Judah encouraged his men, "The conquest of enemies does not come from large armies, but from God's favor." His army fought so bravely and ferociously that the Syrians fled in terror. Judah's warriors pursued them and killed about 800 of them.

When King Antiochus heard of these things, he determined to destroy Jerusalem, and abolish the whole nation. He gave orders to Lysias who delivered 40,000 foot soldiers and 7,000 horsemen to General Ptolemy to defeat the Jews.

> Upon hearing of the large enemy camp, Judah challenged his warriors, "O my fellow soldiers, no other time remains more opportune than the present for courage and contempt of dangers; for if you now fight

Foresight

> manfully, you may recover your liberty."[23]

Judah marched his army of about three thousand men all night to the enemy camp. He commanded the trumpeters to sound for battle and the guerrillas charged into the camp. The surprised and confused enemy could not repel the onslaught and about three thousand died at the hands of Judah's men. Judah

> took a great quantity of gold, and silver, and purple, and blue, and then returned home with joy, and singing hymns to God for their good success; for this victory greatly contributed to the recovery of their liberty.[24]

The Israelite guerrillas continued to fight the Syrians until the Syrians had been overthrown. Then the Jews went to Jerusalem and cleansed the temple from all the filth of the heathen sacrifices of the Zeus worship. They brought in new furniture, offered thank offerings, put bread on the table of show bread and lighted the lamps. Then they rejoiced together with great joy for eight days. From then on, the Jews celebrated this time every year as the Feast of Lights. Today the feast is known as Hanukkah. It is celebrated on the 25th day of Kislev.

~

King Antiochus heard of a very rich city in Persia. The City of Elymais had a very rich temple of Diana full of treasures, weapons and breastplates. They had been left there by Alexander the Great. Desperately in need of funds, the King took his army and besieged Elymais. But the inhabitants drove him away and killed many of his soldiers.

When he was grieving over this loss, someone told him of how the Jews had defeated his commanders. The resulting anxiety threw him into a distemper. He acknowledged that this

> calamity was sent upon him for the miseries he had

---

[23] Josephus - Antiquities of the Jews - Book XII – 7:3
[24] Josephus - Antiquities of the Jews - Book XII – 7:4

The Little Horn

> brought upon the Jewish nation, while he plundered their temple, and contemned their God; and when he had said this, he gave up the ghost.[25]

The *Little Horn* learned too late that it doesn't pay to fight against God. He was the evil one which Daniel saw rising from both the brass-thigh, male-goat, Grecian kingdom and the iron-legs, dreadful-beast, Roman kingdom. The *Little horn* had risen amid the two kingdoms struggling to get the upper hand over each other. But the *stone-cut-from-a-mountain* prevailed and conquered him.

---

[25] Josephus, Antiquities of the Jews 8.1

Foresight

Chapter 20

The Kingdom of God at Hand

It had been about 400 years since Israel last heard the word of the Lord from one they recognized to be a true prophet of God. But now the weathered-skin John the Baptist, dressed in crude camel's hair, stood on the bank of the Jordan River, preaching:

"Repent, for the kingdom of heaven is at hand. For this is he who was spoken of by the prophet Isaiah when he said, the voice of one crying in the wilderness, 'Prepare the way of the Lord; make his paths straight'" (Matthew 3:1-3).

The people showed up en masse with hungry hearts and clung to every word the wilderness orator proclaimed. A Pharisee named Samuel happened to be there. He turned with eyebrows raised to address a Sadducee by the name of Joel next to him. "Well, I am intrigued. It could be that the time is at hand for the stone-cut-from-a-mountain[26] to smash the Roman Empire legs of Nebuchadnezzar's vision, the fourth kingdom he saw. It could be the time for the stone

---

[26] Daniel 2:45

Foresight

to become a mountain to fill the whole earth. Think of it, the kingdom of Israel finally being exalted and flooding the whole earth."

"Well I agree with your implied assessment that Rome is the iron legs of Nebuchadnezzar's vision," declared Joel. "But all things take time. Rome is our friend. I don't want her destroyed just yet. We are going to have to watch out for this John rabble rouser. We don't need to have people stirred against the Roman government and have their leaders get worried and decide to bear down on us."

"What?" cried Samuel. "You want Rome to continue its rule over us? What a treasonous idea."

"Calm down here, Samuel. You know we Sadducees are in good with the Romans. I can clue them in about your attitude."

Samuel glared at Joel with intense hatred written all over his face. He tore his clothes to suggest Joel had just spoken blasphemy and stomped off.

Later, Samuel returned to listen to John. *What awesome words!* he thought to himself. *John preaches from his heart. His anointed words and tone of voice convey to me that he is God's prophet speaking God's word. These great crowds of people who have come out to hear him must feel what I am feeling. The common people are rejoicing. They are repenting of their sins and asking John to baptize them into readiness for the kingdom of God of which he speaks.*

~

The religious leaders, especially the Sadducees, were not so happy. John knew what he was up against. The Sadducees had corrupted the worship of the Lord to their own advantage. The history leading up to their arrival on the scene of action went back to over two hundred years ago. The Maccabees finally drove back the Seleucid armies and cleansed the temple of Zeus worship that Antiochus Epiphanes had imposed on the altars.

These Maccabees, also known as the Hasmonean dynasty, continued to fight for more freedom from the Greek Seleucid rule

The Kingdom of God is at Hand

after they cleansed the temple. Eventually Judah was killed in battle and his brother Jonathan became leader of the rebellion. Simon was the next ruler and his son John Hyrcanus followed him. This John conquered territory to the north and the south and forced the people to choose to either leave their homeland or convert to Judaism. The Hasmoneans became increasingly ruthless. King Alexander Jannacus slaughtered 6,000 of his own people and crucified 800 of the Pharisees who opposed his practices.

Eventually, the Roman Empire usurped authority over the Hasmoneans. This provided an opportunity for the priestly family known as the Sadducees. They played up to the Romans and honored them. In turn, the Romans favored them to have control over the temple worship and office of high priest.

Another religious organization arose to power, calling themselves the Pharisees (the separated ones). They ruled in the governing council along with the Sadducees. They resisted Hellenization as had the Maccabees. They emphasized prayer and study of the law and moral living. But over time they failed to practice what they preached and became hypocritical.

Consequently, the religious and political powers were mostly corrupt. Yet a great number of the common people sought God and cried out for change. They longed for the promised Messiah to deliver them from the mess.

John knew that Herod the Great, the puppet king under the Roman rule, had tried to kill John's cousin, Jesus, when Jesus was a baby. Herod had considered the baby a threat to his hold on the throne. John also knew that the Sadducees were colluding with Herod the Great's son, the present puppet king known as Herod Antipas.

This collusion continued to give the Sadducees their power over the temple worship. And the income from the temple worship provided them with their aristocratic lifestyle. Consequently, Herod and the Sadducees would not take kindly to the idea of a new

Foresight

kingdom being established. They were afraid such a kingdom would attempt to overthrow the Roman government and their positions.

~

Jesus was now thirty years old. He is the Branch of the priesthood, Zechariah heard of in his vision (see Zechariah 3:8-9), arrived on the scene where John was preaching and baptizing. John was baptizing the repentant in preparation for the coming kingdom of which Jesus would be king. When John saw Jesus approaching, he proclaimed:

"Behold, the Lamb of God, who takes away the sin of the world" (John 1:29).

Later, when John baptized Jesus, the Holy Spirit came down from heaven in the form of a dove. It landed on Jesus' head. Simultaneously a voice from heaven said,

"You are my beloved Son; with you I am well pleased" (Luke 3:22).

Then the Spirit led Jesus to the wilderness. There he was tempted for forty days by the devil while eating nothing. At the end of this fast, he became hungry.

The devil said to him, "If you are the Son of God, command this stone to become bread."

And Jesus answered him, "It is written, 'Man shall not live by bread alone.'"

And the devil took him up and showed him all the kingdoms of the world in a moment of time, and said to him, "To you I will give all this authority and their glory, for it has been delivered to me, and I give it to whom I will. If you, then, will worship me, it will all be yours."

And Jesus answered him, "It is written, 'you shall worship the Lord your God, and him only shall you serve.'"

And he took him to Jerusalem and set him on the pinnacle of the temple and said to him, "If you are the Son of God, throw yourself

The Kingdom of God is at Hand

down from here, for it is written, 'He will command his angels concerning you, to guard you, and on their hands they will bear you up, lest you strike your foot against a stone.'"

And Jesus answered him, "It is said, 'You shall not put the Lord your God to the test.'"

And when the devil had ended every temptation, he departed from him until an opportune time (Luke 4:1-13).

* * *

"Well, Satan is up to his old tricks," declared Gabriel.

"Yes, he just applied his three -isms to tempting Jesus," observed Michael. "Tempting Jesus to command the stone to become bread involved the *lust-of-the-flesh sensualism*. Satan tried to divert Jesus from spiritual worship of God by getting Jesus preoccupied with gratifying his senses.

"Showing Jesus the kingdoms of this world involved the *lust-of-the-eyes materialism*. Satan tried to divert Jesus from his focus on being the king of God's kingdom by tempting him to seek kingship of an earthly kingdom. He tried to make Jesus *materialistically* earthly-minded instead of heavenly-minded.

"Suggesting Jesus should cast himself down from the pinnacle of the temple to show off spoke to *the-pride-of-life humanism*. Satan tried to divert Jesus from depending on his Father to glorify him for drawing people to himself. He tried to get Jesus to use a mere human scheme for getting prestige instead."

"Oh, but the evil one miserably failed."

"Yes. Indeed!" declared Michael.

"Well, why did the Spirit lead Jesus into temptation? God does not tempt anyone.

Michael smiled broadly, "Notice God did not tempt Jesus, but he did lead Jesus to this field of temptation for a very important reason.

Foresight

Jesus had to experience the temptations people do so they will be able to relate to him as one of them. This way they will be able to look to him as their high priest."

Now it was Gabriel's turn to smile as his eyes twinkled. "I see. I see. So Jesus is going to serve as high priest in place of Caiaphas, the Sadducee? Caiaphas would not be happy to hear this."

"Well, be assured, he won't know for a while. This is such highly classified intel that none of the other angels know, much less any human being. Certainly, Satan doesn't have a clue."

Gabriel opened his eyes wide and drew in his breath. "Wow. This has to be important information. And I think I might understand. But the thought makes me tremble. Could the Father actually be considering offering Jesus...?"

"Well, remember God asked Abraham to offer his son but intervened at the last moment to prevent the death. Yet I too tremble at what this could mean. But I do know this New Testament history-in-the-making is in the process of revealing a mystery hidden for ages and generations (Colossians 1:26).

Gabriel's eyes opened wide, "What astounding news!"

"Yes. Even now John is about to proclaim some basic revelations."

* * *

Huge crowds continued to rally to hear John. They understood he had been living on a diet of locusts and wild honey. John wore nothing more than a camel's hair garment with a belt of leather about his waist. His burly hair blew downwind toward his audience as he thundered,

"The time is fulfilled, and the kingdom of God is at hand; repent and believe in the gospel" (Mark 1:15).

Just then, he turned to see Jesus walking his way so he cried out,

This brought hope to hearts exasperated with the self-centered corruption of the religious leaders. Their *despair* lifted toward cautious joy. They longed for a visitation from God. John added:

> For from his fullness he offered grace upon grace. For the law was given through Moses; grace and truth came through Jesus Christ (John 1:17).

When Jesus later turned water into wine and began healing the sick, the excitement over this new rabbi knew no bounds. As the Passover of the Jews was about to begin, Jesus went up to Jerusalem. To his horror, he saw people in the Temple exchanging currency and selling oxen, sheep, and pigeons.

Before they knew what was happening, Jesus was coming at them with a whip. He drove them all out of the temple—the people, sheep, and oxen. He dumped out the coins and overturned their tables as he demanded:

> "Take these things away; do not make my Father's house a house of trade" (John 2:16).

Nicodemus looked on with wide eyes and dropped jaw: What audacity. Was no one going to challenge this affront to the accepted practice? Several Sadducees looked on with angry countenances. But something about this usurper spoke authority, and Nicodemus was keen to sense it. Deep-down the Sadducees all know Jesus is right, he acknowledged to himself.

It is wrong for them to be demanding inflated prices for the lambs they sell to those who want to offer Passover lambs to God. And it is wrong for those Jews coming from other countries to be forced to pay a hefty commission to change their currency into temple currency. This wicked scheme of the Sadducees to use what God requires to make themselves rich is a serious affront to the worshipers. It is also a slap in the very face of God. But the consciences of these rulers have long since been seared. I should

Foresight

have done what Jesus just did long ago. But then I probably would not have gotten away with it like Jesus just did.

Nicodemus continued to process: The Sadducees are in collusion with the Roman government which rules our land. They publicly support the Roman government. In return the Roman government gives them authority over the temple worship. And this allows them to take advantage of the people through their sales of sacrificial animals and exchanging money. And even this does not satisfy them. They also charge a temple tax from the worshipers.

The anger with Jesus is so thick it can be felt. But the cowards know that the people know they are being abused. To confront Jesus on this sensitive issue would likely cause a riot in support of what Jesus has done.

Nicodemus smiled broadly. As a Pharisee, he despised the Sadducees and their control of the temple worship. He and some of his fellow Pharisees had to share the rule of the seventy-one member Jerusalem council with the Sadducees. This fact increased his glee at seeing their authority challenged. But competition was not the only issue.

Contrary to so many of the Pharisees, Nicodemus had a heart for God. He had enough spiritual discernment to not just dismiss Jesus. Seeing Jesus leave, he followed him at a distance in hopes of seeing where he was residing. When Jesus entered a house, Nicodemus turned back to keep his duties of meeting with the council.

"What are we going to do with this Jesus?" Caiaphas, the high priest demanded.

"Yes. What are we going to do with this rascal?" chimed in Annas the former high priest.

Nightfall found Nicodemus making his way to the house he saw Jesus enter. Jesus answered his knock on the door and invited him in. Nicodemus began:

> "Rabbi, we know that you are a teacher come from God, for no one can do these signs that you do unless God is with him."
>
> Jesus answered him, "Truly, truly, I say to you, unless one is born again he cannot see the kingdom of God."

The Kingdom of God is at Hand

> Nicodemus said to him, "How can a man be born when he is old? Can he enter a second time into his mother's womb and be born?"
>
> Jesus answered, "Truly, truly, I say to you, unless one is born of water and the Spirit, he cannot enter the kingdom of God. That which is born of the flesh is flesh, and that which is born of the Spirit is spirit. Do not marvel that I said to you, 'You must be born again.' The wind blows where it wishes, and you hear its sound, but you do not know where it comes from or where it goes. So it is with everyone who is born of the Spirit."
>
> Nicodemus said to him, "How can these things be?"
>
> Jesus answered him, "Are you the teacher of Israel and yet you do not understand these things? Truly, truly, I say to you, we speak of what we know, and bear witness to what we have seen, but you do not receive our testimony. If I have told you earthly things and you do not believe, how can you believe if I tell you heavenly things? No one has ascended into heaven except he who descended from heaven, the Son of Man. And as Moses lifted up the serpent in the wilderness, so must the Son of Man be lifted up, that whoever believes in him may have eternal life" (John 3:2-15).

Nicodemus made his way to the door to leave. He thanked Jesus for the conversation and let himself out the door. His mind was full of thought: I have never heard such amazing words. None of the Pharisees have envisioned receiving the Spirit of God as being born of the Spirit. They certainly don't experience such a birth. What an awesome experience to be with Jesus. It seemed like I was in the very presence of God. The atmosphere at once breathed conviction and peace. I cannot say I was ever conscious of being in God's presence before this. Everything I have ever experienced is just about law and duty.

Could God actually become alive to me? Could my spirit ever commune with God's Spirit? Could I have a keen awareness of God and know of his awareness of me like I do with earthly friends? Are we humans only biological until we are born of the spirit? Certainly not. We all have spirits. Evidently, Jesus was implying that our spirits are dead to spiritual reality until we are born

Foresight

of the Spirit. I will have to sleep on this.

Early morning awakened Nicodemus to fresh thinking. He remembered Jesus' words, "The wind blows where it wishes, and you hear its sound, but you do not know where it comes from or where it goes. So it is with everyone who is born of the Spirit." Ah yes, I was conscious of the wind of the Spirit in your presence. I didn't have to know where it was coming from or where it was going to know I felt the Spirit in your presence. I think I am catching on. I can be born of the Spirit without knowing how it happens. I can experience a new spiritual birth. I can be awakened to consciousness of God and the spirit world. Somehow this gives me entrance into the kingdom of God.

It must be that the kingdom of God is more than the kingdom of Israel. It must be a heavenly, spiritual kingdom. Oh. What is this flood of transcendence I now feel? What is this sense of enlightenment? Am I beginning to see, to experience, the kingdom of God as Jesus suggested one could? I think I see this kingdom and its power as being what we Israelites need to experience God. Jesus is the promised Messiah king of this spiritual kingdom. Heavenly Father, I believe in and acknowledge Jesus as the Messiah. I ask you to birth me into a live relationship with you and into citizenship of your kingdom. I repent of all my sins.

Where is this joy and awesome presence coming from? Oh yes. It is the presence of God's Spirit. I don't have to know where it is coming from. But I know. I know. I have become alive in God. Yes. I know I am born again. I am born of the Spirit who now lives in me. I can now have fellowship with God. This relationship with the Lord is what we Israelites need to lift us out of our despair."

* * *

Michael hovered over the crystal glass sea. Gabriel flew in circles around him with his face full of excitement. "Truth and grace are making the difference in a dramatic way," he declared. Jesus brought *truth* to bear on the commercialization of the temple worship."

The Kingdom of God is at Hand

"Absolutely!" replied Michael. "The Sadducees and their merchants were totally at the mercy of Jesus' corrective assault on their scam. And Jesus taught Nicodemus of the *grace* of God for being born again. Truth and grace bring God's kingdom to people to enable them to live for the Lord and conquer all that opposes their walk with him. The dynamics of God's kingdom are coming to people through Jesus even though the kingdom is not yet fully inaugurated in the world."

* * *

Back in Galilee, Jesus cast a demon out of a man, healed a leper, a paralytic, and many sick people. One day Jesus went up to a mountain on the northwestern shore of Galilee. There he prayed all night. In the morning he chose twelve to be his apostles. These included Simon Peter and Andrew his brother. He also chose two other brothers named James and John. In addition to these he chose Philip, Bartholomew, Matthew, Thomas, and James the son of Alphaeus. He also added Simon the Zealot, Judas the son of James (also called Thaddaeus) and Judas Iscariot.

Now thousands were gathering on the hillside to hear him teach. Jesus descended to a level below where the crowd was sitting. There he taught of the *truth*-blessings to be received through *grace* (see Matthew 5). The natural amphitheater carried his strong voice with clearly enunciated words to every listener:

> "Blessed are the poor in spirit, for theirs is the kingdom of heaven" (verse 3).

I can relate to being "poor in spirit" like most of the people here, thought Andrew. We are poor in this world's goods. And I feel my spiritual poverty from lack of receiving God's word in the synagogues. The hypocritical religious leaders only give us dry legalism. Here is the living Word speaking with the anointing of the Spirit to our deep need. How awesome. We can receive the

Foresight

"kingdom of heaven." I sense God giving me faith to believe this.

Peter, Andrew, James, and John sat directly in front of Jesus. Matthew sat behind them and the rest of the apostles sat back a little further. As Jesus said,

> "Blessed are those who mourn, for they shall be comforted" (verse 4),

Matthew thought, I suppose I should mourn my rebellion. I am greatly embittered against the whole temple worship system. This is why I became a tax collector for the Romans. Yet I am glad to be turning from that to follow Jesus. I put my faith in him.

A rich woman named Joanna was inclined to mourn her spiritual lack. I rejoiced at the thought of being comforted in relationship with Jesus, she meditated.

As Jesus said,

> "Blessed are the meek for they shall inherit the earth" (verse 5),

Joanna consented in her heart, I do meekly believe in Jesus. I want to inherit whatever Jesus has for me.

When Jesus proclaimed:

> "Blessed are those who hunger and thirst for righteousness, for they shall be satisfied" (verse 6),

John's eyes glowed as he felt his heart well up in *love* for Jesus. My love for Jesus and his teachings do make me "hunger and thirst" for more.

> Jesus continued: "Blessed are the merciful, for they shall receive mercy" (verse 7).

All right, Matthew thought, I am ready to let go of my bitterness for what life has dealt me in favor of a merciful attitude. I want nothing to hinder me from receiving God's mercy.

> Then Jesus said, "Blessed are the pure in heart for they shall see God" (verse 8).

This is a little too much to grasp, thought Peter. How can I be pure in heart? But I am hungry for more of God.

As Jesus gave the next beatitudes imploring people to be

The Kingdom of God is at Hand

"peacemakers" and to suffer persecution with rejoicing, John thought, This is a little too idealistic to apply to real life. But I am hooked on this new gospel. Perhaps Jesus is the long-promised Messiah who will bring us out of the despair we all feel under the Roman-Sadducee rule.

All the disciples listened in rapt attention as Jesus continued his teaching:

"You have heard it was said, 'You shall love your neighbor and hate your enemy.' But I say to you, Love your enemies and pray for those who persecute you, so that you may be sons of your Father who is in heaven. For he makes his sun rise on the evil and on the good and sends rain on the just and on the unjust. For if you love those who love you, what reward do you have? Do not even the tax collectors do the same?" (Matthew 5:44-46).

Matthew's jaw dropped. He felt the sting of conviction: So Jesus thinks so little of the tax collectors that he uses them as illustration of what one should not be. Is Jesus really my man? I feel the urge to stomp off with the same disgust I have felt for the Pharisees and the Sadducees. This hurts. But it is true. I am not exactly known for being the most loving man. Maybe I should listen on.

"And when you pray, you must not be like the hypocrites. For they love to stand and pray in the synagogues and at the street corners, that they may be seen by others. Truly, I say to you, they have received their reward. But when you pray, go into your room and shut the door and pray to your Father who is in secret. And your Father who sees in secret will reward you.

"And when you pray, do not heap up empty phrases as the Gentiles do, for they think that they will be heard for their many words. Do not be like them, for your Father knows what you need before you ask him. Pray then like this,

"Our Father in heaven, hallowed be your name.
Your kingdom come,
Your will be done,
on earth as it is in heaven.

Foresight

> Give us this day our daily bread,
> and forgive us our debts, as we also
> have forgiven our debtors.
> And lead us not into temptation,
> but deliver us from evil" (Mathew 6:5-13).

Peter raised his eyebrows in thought, Wow. Jesus is sure nailing the Pharisees. They love to pray on the street corners and in the synagogues so people will praise them. And Jesus said we should pray "your kingdom come." John the Baptist told us the kingdom of God is at hand. I am really looking forward to the day Jesus is crowned king of Israel. I look forward to when he throws off this unbearable Roman government. I rejoice to think of him putting the Council composed of Sadducees and Pharisees in their place. Their whole system is so corrupt.

God intends for Israel to be a sovereign nation. He is not pleased to have his people governed by foreign rulers. He expects his people to be led by godly leaders.

"Jesus is setting the stage to overthrow the Roman Government and inaugurate his new kingdom," Peter whispered to John.

"Now Peter, are you sure Jesus' kingdom is going to be an earthly, civil government?"

"Yes. Absolutely. What else could he be talking about?"

John said no more, but Peter's comment had set his thoughts to whirling, We are to pray, "Your kingdom come. Your will be done on earth as it is in heaven." Sounds like his kingdom is going to come through prayer, not military strength, but I guess it could still end up being an earthly kingdom challenging Rome. The future is going to be interesting.

~

Still ministering in Galilee, Jesus healed a centurion's servant of paralysis who was in great pain. He raised a widow's son from the dead and continued to perform many other miracles.

One day he got into a boat and pushed out from the western shore of the Sea of Galilee to teach the multitudes. They had gathered on

The Kingdom of God is at Hand

the rising slopes of the shore. This gave a natural amphitheater and the sea provided a sound back drop to amplify and reverberate his voice to the farthest listener.

Jesus began:

> A sower went out to sow. And as he sowed, some seeds fell along the path, and the birds came and devoured them. Other seeds fell on rocky ground, where they did not have much soil, and immediately they sprang up, since they had no depth of soil, but when the sun rose they were scorched. And since they had no root, they withered away. Other seeds fell among thorns, and the thorns grew up and choked them. Other seeds fell on good soil and produced grain, some a hundredfold, some sixty, some thirty. He who has ears, let him hear" (Matthew 13:3-9).

The bewildered disciples asked for an explanation. Jesus explained: The path-soil persons didn't receive the word so didn't understand. The rocky-soil persons lost out with God after they heard the word because they had no root of serious interest in God. The thorny-soil persons' relationships with God were choked out by the weeds of the cares of this life and the deceitfulness of riches.

* * *

Michael hovered above the crowd and observed, then taught the other angels, "The path-soil people were too bound to their *humanistic* understanding to place *faith* in God. The rocky-soil peoples' hearts were hardened by their love for the world and did not *love* God enough to endure trials. For this reason, they failed to remain true to God when trials came. The thorny-soil people had their *hope* in *materialism* which kept them from retaining their *hope* in God. The good-soil people's hearts were conditioned for *faith, love, and hope* so they produced grain, typical of mature spiritual development. The whole parable points to the need to get serious with

Foresight

God and seek his *truth and grace* instead of living to pleasure the senses with what one sees, hears, tastes, and touches."

* * *

A large crowd was gathering as Jesus resumed teaching with another parable:

grown it is larger than all the garden plants and becomes a tree, that the birds of the air come and make nests in its branches."

Jesu

Peter straightened his frame as he contemplated: How inspiring. I am a part of the kingdom that is going to grow into something big. It will be big enough to support the movers and shakers of society like the branches of a tree support the birds of the air. Jesus certainly has grand plans for the future of his kingdom. Yes, it will expand and influence the culture and politics of the world like leaven permeates the flour into which it is put. The kingdom will rise to dominate the world. Greek Hellenism and Roman rule will be smashed. Jesus truly is the Messiah.

Jesus continued:

"The kingdom of heaven is like treasure hidden in a field, which an found and covered up. Then in his joy he goes and sells all that as and buys that field.

"Again, the kingdom of heaven is like a merchant in search of pearls, who, on finding one pearl of great value, went and sold hat he had and bought it" (Matthew 13:44-45).

Oh, thought John. It is not enough to go for the treasure. One must buy the whole field of God's will. A person cannot just go for the good things God has to offer without buying into God's whole plan for his life. And really, the

The Kingdom of God is at Hand

whole of God's will is like "one pearl of great value." When it is received in its entirety, it provides invaluable, abundant life. What amazing truth of God's grace that Jesus reveals in his parables! How can I not love him?

That evening, Jesus and his disciples got in a boat to cross the sea, and a great windstorm arose with waves crashing water into the boat. But Jesus, exhausted from his teaching, was in the stern, asleep on the cushion. The disciples woke him, and he rebuked the wind and sea into a great calm. When they came to the shore, they stepped out of the boat in the country of the Gadarenes on the eastern shore of the Sea of Galilee. A man came running and fell to the ground before Jesus:

"What have you to do with me, Jesus, Son of the Most High God? I adjure you by God, do not torment me" (Mark 5:7).

Jesus commanded:

"Come out of the man, you unclean spirit" (Mark 5:8).

The demons cried, "Send us into the pigs."

"Go!" Jesus shouted.

The legion of demons sprang from the man into about 2,000 pigs on the cliff nearby. The pigs charged down the steep bank into the sea, gulped the water, and drowned—every one of them.

The herdsmen fled off to tell everybody in the country. Alarm spread. Soon people were flocking to the shore to see the healed man. "We don't know how to handle such miracles." declared one. "Please go back across the sea, Jesus," the people said.

"Let me go with you," cried the healed man to his healer.

"You must stay here," said Jesus. "Spread the word of what I have done for you."

The man became Jesus' first foreign missionary, going throughout the country of the Decapolis preaching to the Gentiles. He stopped anyone who would listen, "I want to tell you what Jesus has done for me. My story will show you that he has power over the forces of darkness. They have to obey his every command."

Foresight

Jesus and his disciples sailed back across the sea to the northwest in the Gennesaret valley. There he healed another demoniac, two blind men, and a woman as she touched his garment. He also sent out his disciples two by two. Even the less-mentioned disciples like Bartholomew, James the son of Alphaeus, and Simon the Zealot preached the gospel. They cast out demons and healed the sick. Even Judas Iscariot participated in the ministry.

After days of this, the disciples caught up with Jesus near Bethsaida, east of where Jesus had commissioned them for their two-by-two ministry. Peter was leading the pack. "We healed the sick and cast out demons." he declared.

A crowd was gathering. Eventually about five thousand men besides women and children were there. The men and women stood. The children sat in front on rocks and the hard ground. All froze in position listening to Jesus' captivating words. Never had any rabbi taught with such a manifest aura of God talking through him. The anointing was even more gripping than the preaching of John the Baptist. Some heads turned slightly to channel an ear toward the flow of words. Others stared in concentration, eyes barely yielding to the urge to blink. Parched souls drank in the words of life.

Jesus taught and responded to questions for hours. When he finally concluded, his heart swelled in compassion for the people. It was now past the evening meal-time. Any town where food could be purchased was a long way off. Jesus turned to James and John. "We need to do something. The people are hungry."

They stared in wide-eyed unbelief at Jesus:

> "This is a desolate place, and the hour is now late. Send them away to go into the surrounding countryside and villages and buy themselves something to eat. Shall we go and buy two hundred denarii worth of bread and give it to them to eat?"

The Kingdom of God is at Hand

> And he said to them, "How many loaves do you have? Go and see." And when they had found out, they said, "Five, and two fish" (Mark 6:35-38).

Jesus spoke to his apostles. "Go out among the people and command them to sit down on the green grass."

"Why are we supposed to sit down?" asked a boy, looking at his mother.

"We shall see."

"This is interesting. I cannot wait to see what this is about," said one man to another.

After giving thanks to the Father, Jesus began breaking the five loaves and dividing the two fish. From his hands, the disciples received the food, distributed it, and came back for more.

"I cannot believe this," declared Peter. "The breaking and dividing never stop. Soon everyone will be full." All the disciples were stunned.

"What a miracle!" many exclaimed.

"What is this awesome, sweet presence I feel?" asked an elderly lady.

"God is here. He cares so much about us that he wants to supply our every need," said her friend. The rest of the crowd ate in silence with their eyes now fixed on Jesus, then on the apostles. They would never be the same.

After twelve baskets were filled with the leftovers Jesus turned his attention to the disciples, "You disciples get back into the boat and head to the eastern shore. I will meet up with you later."

Peter frowned, shrugged his shoulders, and looked at John wide-eyed. "What is Jesus up to now?" his expression said. John silently pursed his lips, raised an eyebrow, and nodded his head toward the boat. They were catching on: just do what the Master says and watch what happens. They got into the boat and launched out.

Oh no! The waves rose, slapping water into the boat. The wind

Foresight

picked up. The disciples were all thinking the same thing: Jesus is not with us to speak calm to the storm. What was he thinking to send us out on the Sea of Galilee at this time? Maybe he doesn't know all things after all. What is this figure coming toward us?

Thomas cried out. "It's a ghost."

"Take heart; it is I. Do not be afraid."

Peter answered him, "Lord, if it is you, command me to come to you on the water."

He said, "Come."

So Peter got out of the boat and walked on the water and came to Jesus. But when he saw the wind, he was afraid, and beginning to sink he cried out, "Lord, save me."

Jesus immediately reached out his hand and took hold of him, saying to him, "O you of little faith, why did you doubt?"

And when they got into the boat, the wind ceased. And those in the boat worshiped him, saying, "Truly you are the Son of God." (Matthew 14:27-33).

Peter remained awe-struck. With his eyes fixed on Jesus, his imagination soared, Not only could Jesus control the wind and the sea, he could change the very composition of the water to enable one to walk on it. What could Jesus not do?

They arrived back at Gennesaret and Jesus healed many various diseases. The faith in Jesus was so strong the people believed they could be healed by touching Jesus' garment, and accordingly they were.

~

Jesus took his disciples and traveled far north of the Sea of Galilee and to the east toward Mt. Hermon. They stopped in Tyre. Jesus needed to get away from the crowds for some rest. But there, a Gentiles woman heard he was in the house and came looking for him. She pled for help and Jesus cast the demon out of her daughter.

The Kingdom of God is at Hand

After a time, Jesus and his disciples returned to the Gentiles land of the Decapolis to the south. They discovered that Jesus' first foreign missionary, the former demoniac, had been faithful in witnessing. The hearts of the people reached out to Jesus. Instead of asking Jesus to leave like they did when the cast-out demons had drowned the near-by pigs, they brought a man who was deaf and had a speech impediment.

> They begged him to lay his hand on him. And taking him aside from the crowd privately, he put his fingers into his ears, and after spitting touched his tongue and looking up to heaven, he sighed and said to him, "Ephphatha," that is, "Be opened." And his ears were opened, his tongue was released, and he spoke plainly (Mark 7:32-35).

Jesus told those who saw this to tell no one but the more he charged them to be quiet, the more zealously they spread the word. People were astonished beyond measure, saying, "He has done all things well. He even makes the deaf hear and the mute speak".

Soon the crowds swarmed him, bringing the blind, the crippled, the mute, and those with other diseases. The people were amazed when they saw the mute speaking, the crippled walking, and the blind seeing. These Gentiles who were so prejudiced against Israel and their God, now glorified Jesus with the highest praise. What a change of attitude from the last time he had been here!

Eventually, 4,000 men besides women and children were gathered. Jesus was as eager to feed these Gentiles as he had been to feed the 5,000 Jews.

James said, "We have loaves and a few small fish."

As the food multiplied, all ate until they were satisfied. Then they gathered up seven baskets of fragments which were left over.

* * *

Foresight

"I am intrigued," said Gabriel to Michael as they both hovered over the scene.

"At the miracle of feeding the crowd with seven loaves and a few fish?" questioned Michael.

"Well of course, but I expected that miracle after seeing Jesus feed the 5,000. What fascinates me is some trivia in the two miraculous feedings."

"Oh?"

"Yes. How many baskets remained after the feeding of the 5,000?

"Twelve."

"Exactly. And after this feeding of the 4,000, seven baskets remained."

"I see where you are going Gabriel. The twelve could represent the twelve tribes of the Jews who were fed in the feeding of the 5,000. And the seven could represent the seven Canaanite nations, the seven nations Joshua drove out of the land of Canaan. The people of Decapolis whom Jesus just fed are the descendants of these nations."

"Yes Michael. Evidently Jesus likes to hide some interesting, meaningful trivia in his miracles and teachings. He likes to hide it for those who are seeking the *truth*," Gabriel concluded.

"Yes Gabriel. This bit of trivia strongly suggests that Jesus is as interested in the Gentiles as he is the Jews. He is even interested in all the details of their existence. It will take some doing to convince the proud Jews of this reality."

* * *

Jesus took his disciples back up north to Caesarea Philippi. At the Pagan Shrine called the Gates of Hell, Jesus asked,

"Who do people say that the Son of Man is?"

And they said, "Some say John the Baptist, others say Elijah, and

The Kingdom of God is at Hand

others Jeremiah or one of the prophets."

He said to them, "But who do you say that I am?"

Simon Peter replied, "You are the Christ, the Son of the living God."

And Jesus answered him, "Blessed are you, Simon Bar-Jonah. For flesh and blood has not revealed this to you, but my Father who is in heaven. And I tell you, you are Peter, and on this rock I will build my church" (Matthew 16:13-18).

Jesus turned and pointed to the shrine:

"And the gates of hell shall not prevail against it. I will give you the keys of the kingdom of heaven, and whatever you bind on earth shall be bound in heaven, and whatever you loose on earth shall be loosed in heaven" (Matthew 16:18-19).

"However, I want you to tell no one that I am the Christ. Yet because I am, I must go to Jerusalem. I must suffer many things from the religious leaders there and be killed and be raised on the third day."

Peter frowned and glared at his Master. When Jesus was finished speaking, Peter said, "Please come aside so I can talk with you privately."

Jesus complied. When they were out of earshot from the rest of the disciples, Peter pleaded, "Jesus, please don't discourage us any more with this talk of dying." Peter stressed:

"Far be it from you, Lord. This shall never happen to you."

Jesus turned to him with piercing eyes: "Get behind me, Satan. You are a hindrance to me. For you are not setting your mind on the things of God, but on the things of man" (Matthew 16:22-23).

When they returned to the rest of the disciples Jesus said to them:

"If anyone would come after me, let him deny himself and take up his cross and follow me. For whoever would save his life will lose it, but whoever loses his life for my sake will find it. For what will it

Foresight

profit a man if he gains the whole world and forfeits his soul? Or what shall a man give in return for his soul? For the Son of Man is going to come with his angels in the glory of his Father, and then he will repay each person according to what he has done. Truly, I say to you, there are some standing here who will not taste death until they see the Son of Man coming in his kingdom" (Matthew 16:24-28).

Peter mused, Since Jesus is going to come in his kingdom before some here die, what Jesus said about being killed and resurrected can only mean that the religious leaders want to kill him. He isn't going to actually die a physical death. This could not be. There would be no reason for him to die.

Anyway, Jesus declares he will set up his kingdom in this generation. This is what we need. The nasty Roman government must be destroyed. Israel must reign supreme above the nations. Jesus positively confirms that he is the Christ, the King. What a day this will be when he finally puts his enemies down and vindicates me and his other disciples for standing with him.

~

It was the fall of the year and Jesus and his disciples went to Jerusalem for the Feast of Tabernacles.

About the middle of the feast Jesus went up into the temple and began teaching. The Jews therefore marveled, saying, "How is it that this man has learning, when he has never studied?"

So Jesus answered them, "My teaching is not mine, but his who sent me. If anyone's will is to do God's will, he will know whether the teaching is from God or whether I am speaking on my own authority. The one who speaks on his own authority seeks his own glory; but the one who seeks the glory of him who sent him is true, and in him there is no falsehood. Has not Moses given you the law? Yet none of you keeps the law. Why do you seek to kill me?" (John 7:14-18).

James looked over at Peter. Peter's facial expression said, "Here

The Kingdom of God is at Hand

we go again. He is still talking about being killed."

James dropped his head and shook it from side to side as if to say, "I don't know what to make of this!"

> On the last day of the feast, the great day, Jesus stood up and cried out, "If anyone thirsts, let him come to me and drink. Whoever believes in me, as the Scripture has said, 'Out of his heart will flow rivers of living water'" (John 7:37-38).

A huge controversy arose over Jesus. Some said he was demon possessed or insane. Others said this could not be true because such a person could not open the eyes of the blind.

The chief priest and the Pharisees sent officers to take Jesus. The officers became enraptured with Jesus' teachings. The more they listened the more they knew Jesus was no usual man. Their hungry hearts longed to welcome him into their lives. Finally, they returned without him. The Pharisees asked why they did not arrest Jesus. They answered:

> "No one ever spoke like this man!" (John 7:46).

Jesus continued to teach. One of the amazing things he said was:

> "I am the good shepherd. The good shepherd lays down his life for the sheep. For this reason the Father loves me, because I lay down my life that I may take it up again" (John 10:11).

"This confirms my belief that Jesus is talking of giving his life in terms of giving all his energy and abilities to become the king of Israel," said Peter to James and John. "A good shepherd will do all he can to protect his sheep and provide a good life for him. But I have never known of one to actually die doing so. Jesus doesn't really mean he will physically die. He is just showing us how seriously he takes the responsibility of bringing our nation out of its present Roman oppression. He is devoting his whole life to the cause. And in doing so, he lays down his life."

"How can you be so sure?" asked John. "I shudder every time the Master talks this way."

Foresight

"Never fear," pronounced Peter. "Just as the Father has revealed to me that Jesus is the Christ—Jesus commended me for this, you know—I discern the true meaning of Jesus' prophecy on this matter. Jesus will give his all to become our king, but he doesn't have to physically die. After all, dying would accomplish nothing but please his enemies and make them gloat over his demise."

"Well, I hope you are right," declared James.

~

It was winter and Jesus and his disciples went to the Feast of Dedication. As Jesus was walking in the colonnade of Solomon in the temple certain people gathered around and asked:

"How long will you keep us in suspense? If you are the Christ, tell us plainly." Jesus answered them, "I told you, and you do not believe. The works that I do in my Father's name bear witness about me, but you do not believe because you are not among my sheep. My sheep hear my voice, and I know them, and they follow me. I give them eternal life, and they will never perish, and no one will snatch them out of my hand. My Father, who has given them to me, is greater than all, and no one is able to snatch them out of the Father's hand. I and the Father are one" (John 10:22-30).

The Jews picked up stones. "We are going to stone you for blasphemy, because you, being a man, make yourself God," they shouted. But Jesus slipped out of their hands.

* * *

"What? Jesus is truly God. What devastating news. God has pulled a fast one on us. No wonder Jesus seems to not be fazed by the exceedingly fierce temptations I bring to him. This is not playing by the rules," cried Satan.

"Hold on Superior Evil One," shouted Pan. "Jesus is trying to get

The Kingdom of God is at Hand
all to believe he is God and you are gullible enough to believe what he says. Don't you remember that Jesus was born of Mary in Bethlehem in the manger? He is only a man."

"Oh, yes. Wow. I about fell for that one."

"What do you mean? You totally swallowed that line."

"Nah. I was just being overly cautious, but what Jesus is claiming can have devastating effects. If people believe he is truly God, equal to God the Father, they will worship him and go along with all his strategies to defeat us. This will be hard to resist."

"Well, just leave it to me and Ares. We will marshal all the religious leaders and the Romans to crucify this one who says he is God. Yes, just putting a sword through him is not enough. We will crucify him so he can hang in shame before the whole world."

A hellish grin spread across Satan's face. "Well, I must say your hate-filled passion inspires me. Yes Pan. By all means, muster all the demons of hell, especially all the demons we have appointed to be Greek gods. You and they already have a strong foothold in the society through the Roman influence. Start with the religious leaders. They are the most susceptible. They already hate Jesus without our help."

Pan produced a crooked, sneering smile. "And we will solicit Judas also. He already is following our lead. The thief will be fascinated with the clever plot we propose."

"Whatever. Just proceed with the slimiest, dirtiest, low-down scheme you can come up with."

"We are on our way," cried Pan and Ares.

* * *

Jesus continued to do many miracles of healing throughout the land. He even raised his close friend Lazarus from the dead. On his

Foresight

last journey to Jerusalem Jesus healed ten lepers in a village and taught his disciples to always pray and not lose heart.

He continued to teach the Gospel *truth* and offer his *grace*. The *truth* brought the Gospel with all of the amazing blessings of its salvation message. *Grace* applied the forgiveness that *truth* offered. It gave power to live out the will of God which *truth* taught. As *the truth* would continue to be revealed, it would show *the way* to *the life*, abundant life. This is why Jesus would say,

> "I Am the Way, and the Truth, and the Life" (John 14:1 & 6).

Jesus would declare the truth to be the word of God. He would teach the people to live out the *word of God* and the *testimony* of what he does for them through the Word.

Chapter 21

Passover to the Lord's Supper

On this Friday Jesus and his disciples arrived in Bethany, at Lazarus's house on the east side of the Mount of Olives on the east side of Jerusalem. They came here to be close to the Passover celebration which they would attend.

The stalwart Lazarus, recently raised from the dead, was outside sitting on a log looking youthful and healthy. He jumped to his feet at the sight of the new arrivals. "Welcome friends. How good it is to see you!" he bellowed.

Mary and Martha rushed out from the house.

"Jesus, Jesus, Peter, John, Thomas, James, Bartholomew; all of you. Welcome. Welcome. Welcome," cried Martha.

"Welcome. Welcome," Mary said. "Come inside. Let me wash your feet. You have come a long way. I know you are weary, and Sabbath is about to begin."

Martha brought out loaves of bread for all to eat. Mary washed all the disciples' feet. Then she stepped out of the room for a moment and came back with tears streaming down her face.

Foresight

Mary approached Jesus with a vessel holding a full pound of expensive ointment made from pure nard. She freely poured out the whole contents on Jesus' feet and spread it across his feet with her hair. The fragrance permeated the atmosphere.

Mary lingered with Jesus. She had poured out her bridal ointment. It was what every young woman saved up for the day she would be married. She seemed to be saying, "I am going to forfeit earthly marriage to be married to your service."

Her thoughts were on the unbearable news she had heard, Can what I have heard be true? The powers want to crucify you? Crucify you my Lord? The thought is too horrifying for words. But I will be married to your service, or be a memorial to your death if you die.

The tears came in torrents as her body trembled with sobs, Are these feet soon going to be pierced with the cruel spikes? she agonized in her mind.

> But Judas Iscariot, who was about to betray the Lord, said, "Why was this ointment not sold for three hundred denarii and given to the poor?" He said this, not because he cared about the poor, but because he was a thief, and having charge of the moneybag he used to help himself to what was put into it.
>
> Jesus said, "Leave her alone, so that she may keep it for the day of my burial. For the poor you always have with you, but you do not always have me" (John 12:4-8).

The next morning Judas rose late after the rest were on their way to Jerusalem, He groaned with aching body and soul as he sat up and rubbed his eyes. He had barely slept all night.

Troubling thoughts were driving him mad: What was the anointing of Jesus' feet last night all about? And why was Jesus talking of his burial? He seemed focused on death rather than being a champion for the cause of liberating Israel. But the way he rebuked me before everyone was the final straw. Oh. What a put down! What an embarrassment!

I will have my revenge and make some money in the process. I think the religious leaders will be glad to work with me. Anyway, if Jesus is truly the

Passover to the Lord's Supper

Messiah, they won't be able to take him. He has avoided other attempts on his life. If he is the Messiah this will force him to publicly demonstrate himself superior to all the forces coming against him. Then everyone will know he is the Messiah.

The large crowd at the feast heard that Jesus was coming to Jerusalem:

> So they took branches of palm trees and went out to meet him, crying out, "Hosanna! Blessed is he who comes in the name of the Lord, even the King of Israel!"
>
> And Jesus found a young donkey and sat on it, just as it is written, "Fear not, daughter of Zion; behold, your king is coming, sitting on a donkey's colt!" (John 12:13-15).

The crowd was beyond jubilant with their thoughts, Surely the Messiah is here! Many were thinking: This reminds us of the time when the Maccabees repossessed the temple and cleansed it. On that day the people were

> carrying green palm branches and sticks decorated with ivy, they paraded around, singing grateful praises to him who had brought about the purification of his own Temple.[27]

Today the palm branches we wave speak of a similar hope, but an even greater one. Jesus the performer of miracles, the resurrector of Lazarus, is riding on a donkey toward the temple. He has to be the Messiah, the promised King. "Hosannah. Hosannah. Hosannah. Hosanna! (Save. Oh save.)," the people cried.

Then they broke out in song with the Psalm known as "the Egyptian Hallel:"

> The stone that the builders rejected
>   has become the cornerstone.
> This is the Lord's doing;
>   it is marvelous in our eyes.

---

[27] 2 Maccabees 10:7

Foresight

> This is the day that the Lord has made;
>   let us rejoice and be glad in it.
> Save us, we pray, O Lord!
>   O Lord, we pray, give us success!
> Blessed is he who comes in the name of the Lord!
>   We bless you from the house of the Lord.
> The Lord is God,
>   and he has made his light to shine upon us.
> Bind the festal sacrifice with cords,
>   up to the horns of the altar!
> You are my God, and I will give thanks to you;
>   you are my God; I will extol you.
> Oh give thanks to the Lord, for he is good;
>   for his steadfast love endures forever! (Psalm 118:22-29).

Hosannah. Hosannah. Hosannah. Hosannah. Hosannah. Hosannah. Hosannah.

The Pharisees said to each other,

> "You see that you are gaining nothing. Look, the world has gone after him" (John 12:19).

Monday, the following day, was time for another Maccabees-like cleansing of the temple. The spirit of yesterday's celebration seemed to demand it. Jesus went into action as soon as he entered the temple. He drove out those who sold as he cried,

> "It is written, 'My house shall be a house of prayer,' but you have made it a den of robbers" (Luke 19:46).

After this he taught daily in the temple. All the while the chief priests, scribes, and other leaders were seeking to destroy him. But they stalled, because the people were hanging on his every word.

~

Jesus took his disciples to the temple. Standing in the court, He surveyed the glamorous edifice with casual interest. Then he left the

Passover to the Lord's Supper

temple and was going away. But his disciples called him back to point out the buildings of the temple. Jesus stretched out his hands toward the temple with a sweeping gesture, "You see all these, do you not? Truly, I say to you, there will not be left here one stone upon another that will not be thrown down" (Matthew 24:2).

The disciples looked at each other with stunned expressions and thoughts along these lines: Why is Jesus disregarding the temple, the monument to Israel's greatness and covenant relationship with Almighty God? We have always understood the temple to be an indestructible testimony to the world of Israel's high regard for God and his high regard for our nation.

Zechariah declared that the word of the Lord to Zerubbabel was a command to build this house. The prophets considered the building of the temple to be an expression of Israel's determination to worship God and follow him. And even though Herod was a wicked man, God used his architectural genus to greatly expand and beautify the house Zerubbabel built. To disregard the temple seems seriously unpatriotic and even irreverent.

Jesus began to tell of a time of great distress, tribulation, and the end of the current age. He said the Son of Man will come:

"And he will send out his angels with a loud trumpet call, and they will gather his elect from the four winds, from one end of heaven to the other. Truly, I say to you, this generation will not pass away until all these things take place" (Matthew 24:31, 35).

Peter's eyes widened and his jaw dropped. Oh yes. Jesus did say something about this soon after he began his ministry. Yes. He said, "Destroy this temple, and in three days I will raise it up" (John 2:19).

Is Jesus actually going to build another temple grander than this one? Everything Jesus is saying recently just seems far out. Everything is becoming a blur.

∼

Jesus and his disciples spent time with Lazarus, Mary, and Martha during Passover week. This evening was Tuesday. Everyone was looking forward to 6:00 on the Thursday evening (the beginning

Foresight

of Jewish Friday the fourteenth day of the first month of the Jewish year). This was the time the Passover lambs would be slain. Then each family group would eat one of the lambs for the evening meal. This commemorated the lamb's blood put on the doorposts and lintels in Egypt to save them from the death angel. In this way, Passover reminded them that blood had to be shed to provide salvation.

Jesus looked at his disciples with compassionate, loving eyes. How unprepared they are! he thought. They are like sheep about to be scattered when the moment comes. He said to them,

"You know that after two days the Passover is coming, and the Son of Man will be delivered up to be crucified" (Matthew 26:2).

The disciples looked down and several sighed deeply. Is Master losing his bearings? Is he losing the sense of who he is? The Messiah is supposed to be encouraging everyone to stand strong and to expect the best. He is supposed to project optimism and greatness. Why all this talk about dying, and now crucifixion. What shame this would bring if it were to happen.

Peter, James, and John closed their eyes as if trying to close out the horrendous picture: Surely Jesus is not going to be crucified literally. He must be speaking in symbolic language. He cannot die physically if he is going to proclaim himself to be the Messiah when the time is right.

Jesus saw the effect. How he desired to open their minds and hearts to accept the truth and then give them grace to bear it, but their hearts are hard. They wanted victory their own way. Sadly, their present outlook would have to meet total disappointment in order for them to find *hope* in God's *truth* and *grace*.

The next morning Peter rose early before the rest with his mind on a mission. His jaw was set as he mulled serious thoughts: If the powers should try to crucify Jesus, I am going to be ready. He got there just in time to see burly, brawny Elam the blacksmith at the door unlocking his shop for the day.

"I need a sword, Elam."

"What? I thought you were a man of peace."

"Sometimes even a man of peace needs a sword," Peter

Passover to the Lord's Supper

explained.

Elam shuffled over to his bench and picked up a sword lying there. "Here is one that won't set you back too much."

Peter took it and felt the weight. "I think I might like the one over there hanging on the wall better. It appears to be more finely crafted."

Elam reached over and retrieved it from the hook.

"Ah. This fits my hand better and is not so heavy. I can really wield this one."

"By the way, you wouldn't be preparing to defend your Master, would you? One man against many won't stand a chance. I doubt that the high priest will send any less than a small garrison."

"What? Have you heard that they are going to take Jesus? I have been thinking I should be ready in case, but evidently you know they are going to take him?"

"Yes, I hear a lot of talk here, you know. Both the Sadducees and the Pharisees are really mad. I have a feeling you are going to feel called upon to use a sword, but what can you do by yourself?"

"Didn't Jonathan and his armor bearer defeat a whole garrison? If a man has his mind set and enough faith in God, he can defeat any onslaught."

Elam's eyes widened, "Wow. I guess you are serious. This sword costs twice the money of the other one."

"Fine. I will gladly pay."

~

Jesus taught in the temple as the religious leaders challenged his knowledge and teachings.

Sadducees came to him, who say that there is no resurrection, and they asked him a question, saying, "Teacher, Moses said, 'If a man dies having no children, his brother must marry the widow and raise up offspring for his brother.' Now there were seven brothers among us. The first married and died, and having no offspring left his wife to his brother. So too the second and third, down to the seventh. After them all, the woman died. In the resurrection, therefore, of the seven, whose wife will she be? For they all had her."

But Jesus answered them, "You are wrong, because you know neither the Scriptures nor the power of God. For in the resurrection they neither marry nor are given in marriage but are like angels in heaven. And as for the resurrection of the dead, have you not read what was said to you by God, 'I am the God of Abraham, and the God of Isaac, and the God of Jacob?' He is not God of the dead, but of the living."

And when the crowd heard it, they were astonished at his teaching. But when the Pharisees heard that he had silenced the Sadducees, they gathered together. And one of them, a lawyer, asked him a question to test him. "Teacher, which is the great commandment in the Law?"

And he said to him, "You shall love the Lord your God with all your heart and with all your soul and with all your mind. This is the great and first commandment. And a second is like it, you shall love your neighbor as yourself. On these two commandments depend all the Law and the Prophets" (Matthew 24:23-40).

John looked at Thomas, "What amazing insight Jesus gives into the scriptures. I never thought about the ten commandments and all the law being about love."

"Well, you think about it, the first four of the Ten Commandments are about loving God. The last six are about loving our neighbors, our fellow people," observed Thomas.

"Very good. Very good. You always have been quite the thinker."

"Well John, I don't think there is any love being lost on Jesus. The Sadducees and the Pharisees are not trying to arrive at truth with their questions. They hate Jesus and are simply trying to get him to say something which would mark him as a false teacher."

"Not working too well is it?"

Passover to the Lord's Supper

"Not really. Nobody has ever cornered Jesus on his teachings from the scriptures."

"Yes, Thomas. Why should anyone expect to outwit the Son of Man, God himself in human flesh?"

"Is he really the promised Son of Man, the Messiah?"

"Thomas. How dare you?"

"If only I knew for sure. Would the Messiah be headed for the cross?"

"Oh, Thomas."

~

Jesus sent Peter and John out to prepare for the day of Unleavened Bread, saying:

> "Go and prepare the Passover for us, that we may eat it."
>
> They said to him, "Where will you have us prepare it?"
>
> He said to them, "Behold, when you have entered the city, a man carrying a jar of water will meet you. Follow him into the house that he enters and tell the master of the house, 'The Teacher says to you, "Where is the guest room, where I may eat the Passover with my disciples? And he will show you a large upper room furnished; prepare it there'" (Luke22:8-12).

The brothers obeyed and were amazed. Everything happened as Jesus said it would. Then they prepared the Passover.

~

Jesus passed around the first of the four traditional cups of Passover,[28] the Cup of Sanctification.[29] Then Jesus pointed out Judas as the one who would betray him, and Judas fled the room. Next, Jesus washed the disciples' feet to demonstrate the importance of being servants.

---

[28] Mishnah Pesachim 10,1
[29] Moishe Rosen, *Christ in the Passover* (Moody Publishers, Chicago) 126

Foresight

Then he passed the second cup for them all to drink, the Cup of Praise[30] or Forgiveness.[31] They all ate the bitter herbs and the lamb.[32] Jesus broke the unleavened bread and passed it out as he said,

> "This is my body, which is for you. Do this in remembrance of me" (1 Corinthians 11:24).

Then he passed out the third cup, the Cup of Redemption,[33] saying,

> "This cup is the new covenant in my blood. Do this, as often as you drink it, in remembrance of me. For as often as you eat this bread and drink the cup, you proclaim the Lord's death until he comes" (1 Corinthians 11:25-26).

John leaned back farther in his reclining position and covered his eyes with his hand. His thoughts were in a whirl. I guess Jesus is not going to serve the fourth cup of the traditional Passover meal, the Cup of Acceptance.[34]

But this is not the only mystery. Jesus asked us to drink of the wine as a metaphor of his blood and to eat of the bread as a metaphor of his body. According to custom, when one accepts a covenant, he drinks from the cup of the person who offers the contract. The cup signifies that he is willing to drink the life the covenant offers.

According to this custom, Jesus must be asking us to accept his covenant and he may be alluding to a marriage covenant. A bride signifies her acceptance of the bridegroom's proposed marriage covenant by drinking a cup of wine. This means she is accepting the life together with the groom that his proposed covenant offers.

---

[30] Moishe Rosen, *Christ in the Passover* (Moody Publishers, Chicago) 136
[31] Michal E. Hunt, *Jesus and the Mystery of the Tamid Sacrifice* (Thomas Nelson Publishers for Ignatius Press) Loc 2885
[32] Josephus, (Wars of the Jews) 6.9.3
[33] Moishe Rosen, *Christ in the Passover* (Moody Publishers, Chicago) 139
Michal E. Hunt, *Jesus and the Mystery of the Tamid Sacrifice* (Thomas Nelson Publishers for Ignatius Press) Loc 2885
[34] Michal E. Hunt, *Jesus and the Mystery of the Tamid Sacrifice* (Thomas Nelson Publishers for Ignatius Press) Loc 2885

Passover to the Lord's Supper

But we have not been offered a covenant—well now, wait a minute. What about when Mother came to Jesus asking him to grant what she would ask, and Jesus answered,

> "What do you want?"
>
> She said to him, "Say that these two sons of mine are to sit, one at your right hand and one at your left, in your kingdom."
>
> Jesus answered, "You do not know what you are asking. Are you able to drink the cup that I am to drink?" (Matthew 20:21-22).

And James and I answered, "We are able" (Matthew 20:22).

So at least James and I are locked in. But really, I would not have it any other way. I hope the kingdom of God is not far away but apparently it holds some surprises. What about this matter of eating his body and drinking his blood as Jesus talked about some time ago? He said,

> "Truly, truly, I say to you, unless you eat the flesh of the Son of Man and drink his blood, you have no life in you" (John 6:53).

Regardless of what this all means, things seem to be shaping up for the kingdom of God to soon be here.

Jesus led the disciples in the last traditional event of the Passover meal, singing a portion of the Hallel:[35]

> The stone that the builders rejected
>   has become the cornerstone.[a]
> This is the Lord's doing;
>   it is marvelous in our eyes.
> This is the day that the Lord has made;
>   let us rejoice and be glad in it.
> Save us, we pray, O Lord!
>   O Lord, we pray, give us success!
> Blessed is he who comes in the name of the Lord!
>   We bless you from the house of the Lord.

---

[35] The Mishnah Pesachim 10:7 indicates they sang the Hallel for the Passover meal. I cannot say which portion of the Hallel they sang. This portion seems likely.

Foresight

> The Lord is God,
> and he has made his light to shine upon us. (Psalm 118:22-27).

Chapter 22

The Hellish Plot

"The time has come to proceed with the slimiest, dirtiest, lowdown scheme ever concocted by any fiend of hell," pronounced Pan. "I am proud to own this scheme as my own. Satan authorized it, but my smarts invented it. And now my brilliance will direct and inspire everyone for action. Between my brain power and Ares' blood lust directing this operation, we are as good as having Jesus on the cross right now.

"We must focus on filling spirits with darkness and confusion. This will keep them from rallying around Jesus."

"Yes. Yes. Yes," the imps all screamed.

"Wow. This is terrific," cried Aphrodite. "You are the one to lead us. I am at your service."

"We are at your service," cried the other devils.

"Ok. Now listen. Jesus has made great strides in awakening people. Most of the common people are wholly enraptured with him. They hang on to his every word. And this fascination has the potential to open their hearts to being spiritually born again. This would make

Foresight

them spiritually alive, and greatly aware of God. I hate to voice this reality. But we must face it to pollute the atmosphere of the spiritual realm with darkness until people get totally confused. They will all turn from their devotion to Jesus to actually getting a thirst for his blood, thanks to our clever Ares."

"All of them?" asked Eros with a skeptical voice.

"Well. Probably not all of them but enough to create a mob movement. You wait and see," replied Pan.

Pan continued, "Now to fully facilitate and administrate this endeavor, I need to appoint some of you to focus on specifics besides just generally creating darkness and confusion. Aphrodite, you need to become all about greed. You have already inspired Judas to embezzle money from the funds for Jesus' ministry. And you have driven him to plot with the chief priests to betray Jesus for money. But now you must totally possess him to drive him to follow through with the deed.

"Gaia, you must become a specialist in jealousy and ramp up your efforts. It is not enough to just get the religious leaders to try to trick Jesus into answering their questions with something they can use to condemn him. That has backfired on us anyway. Get them so jealous of Jesus that they will accuse him of blasphemy. You will need lots of help. I commission you with authority to draft all the demons you will need to possess every antichrist Sadducee and Pharisee. Fully inflame them with jealousy.

"Dionysus, you must specialize in confusion. I commission you with authority to draft several thousand demons to confuse the common people. Get them to focus on the fact that Jesus has not taken advantage of their adoration to proclaim himself king. Make them feel betrayed.

"Ares and I will drive Herod and Pilate mad with fear of losing their positions and influence. All of the rest of you will simply be alert to opportunities. Create confusion and anger in every person who has the potential to contribute to a mob spirit. Let me find no one being idle. If you are presently occupied with other wicked pursuits, put them on hold. Direct all of your energies to this campaign to put Jesus on a cruel cross.

"Artemis, you must bend your focus to creating mass discouragement in the disciples. You remember that our ultimate goal is to drive them to *despair*."

"Well, okay. I will do my best. But I am not sure God is going to let us get by with all of this. He could stop us you know," replied Artemis.

"Artemis. How dare you bring up that awful reality? Now get away from me, all of you, and get to work!" screamed Pan.

Foresight

Chapter 23

World Crisis

Before leaving the upper room, Jesus taught powerful truths with great love and tenderness to his disciples. They would always remember that he pronounced, "I am the way, and the truth, and the life. No one comes to the Father except through me" (John 14:6).

After they left, Jesus continued teaching as they walked:

> "I tell you the truth, it is to your advantage that I go away, for if I do not go away, the Helper will not come to you. But if I go, I will send him to you. And when he comes, he will convict the world concerning sin and righteousness and judgment, concerning sin, because they do not believe in me; concerning righteousness, because I go to the Father, and you will see me no longer; concerning judgment, because the ruler of this world is judged" (John 16:7-11).

Jesus paused for these truths to sink in. John, the disciple who had the most intimate friendship with Jesus shook his head to try to comprehend, *Jesus keeps talking about dying and now he is talking about going to the Father. But who is this helper and what is his conviction all about?*

* * *

Foresight

Michael and Gabriel were flying overhead. They were closely guarding the disciples' minds from Pan's campaign of confusion. "It will be the Holy Spirit who will come and convict," said Michael to Gabriel.

"As Jesus said, First, he will convict the unbelieving of sin. This will be about *faith*. This helper will convict people to believe, to have *faith* in Jesus.

"Second, the helper will also convict of righteousness because the Lord is going away, and the disciples will no longer see him. To behold Christ is to *love* him and his righteous character. But in his absence the Holy Spirit will pour out godly *love* in the hearts of Jesus' followers. This will cause them to *love* him in the context of his righteousness.

"And lastly, the helper will convict of judgment, because the ruler of this world is to be judged. The ruler of this world is to be judged to have no rightful claim on souls. For Jesus will have made the final sacrifice for their sin. What awesome *hope* this will bring! Satan the ruler of this world will be put down."

"Great observation," declared Gabriel.

＊＊＊

Jesus continued his teaching:

"I still have many things to say to you, but you cannot bear them now. When the Spirit of truth comes, he will guide you into all the truth, for he will not speak on his own authority, but whatever he hears he will speak, and he will declare to you the things that are to come. He will glorify me, for he will take what is mine and declare it to you. All that the Father has is mine; therefore I said that he will take what is mine and declare it to you" (John 16:12-15).

World Crisis

Oh. So the helper is the Spirit of truth, thought Peter. Jesus whom we can see with our eyes is going to be replaced by a spirit whom we cannot see? Well this is not too reassuring. If only Jesus would come out of this death wish. If only he would take advantage of the political opportunity to proclaim himself King. Then we would be on track for deliverance from the Roman government that oppresses us. I am afraid our Lord has lost his bearings, and we his disciples are going to pay a high price for following him. Come to think of it, our lives are going to be in danger also. Those who want to kill Jesus will certainly be after us also. We are a part of the Jesus movement.

Jesus went on speaking but it tended to be overload for the disciples. Yet the angels were there to block the surrounding darkness from distracting them. And as they did this, they burned the message into the disciple's memories for future understanding.

Jesus ended the teaching with these words:

> "Behold, the hour is coming, indeed it has come, when you will be scattered, each to his own home, and will leave me alone. Yet I am not alone, for the Father is with me. I have said these things to you, that in me you may have peace. In the world you will have tribulation. But take heart; I have overcome the world" (John 16:32-33).

By now Jesus and his disciples had come near the Garden of Gethsemane. Jesus called them to stand in a circle. Then he looked up to heaven and prayed in their presence (John 17):

> "Father, the hour has come. Glorify your Son so that the Son may glorify you, since you gave him authority over all flesh.... Father, glorify me in your own presence with the glory that I had with you before the world existed." (verses 1-5).

Yes, thought Peter. Father, glorify your Son by inspiring him to take authority over the forces that are coming against him.

> Jesus continued, "I have revealed your name to the people you gave me from the world. They have believed that you sent me" (verses 6-8).

Foresight

Yes indeed, thought James. We have believed. If only you would declare yourself King of Israel and put down all forces against you, then our faith would be increased.

Jesus prayed on:

> "I pray for them. I am not praying for the world but for those you have given me, because they are yours. Everything I have is yours, and everything you have is mine, and I am glorified in them. I am no longer in the world, but they are in the world, and I am coming to you. Holy Father, protect them by your name that you have given me, so that they may be one as we are one… I do not ask that you take them out of the world, but that you keep them from the evil one" (verses 9-15).

Yes, thought Philip. We need the Father's protection. Now invoke the Father's power against the high priest, the chief priests, the Pharisees and the Sadducees. Stop their plans to kill you now.

> "They are not of the world, just as I am not of the world. Sanctify them by the truth; your word is truth. As you sent me into the world, I also have sent them into the world. I sanctify myself for them, so that they also may be sanctified by the truth" (verses 17-19).

Peter set his jaw as he declared to himself, Yes, the Father is even now sanctifying me to the cause of defending you. My sword is ready. My courage is strong like Jonathan's of old. In spite of these rash thoughts, he listened carefully to the rest as Jesus continued his prayer,

> "I pray not only for these, but also for those who believe in me through their word. May they all be one, as you, Father, are in me and I am in you…so that the world may know that you sent me and loved them even as you loved me" (verses (20-23).

This is too much, thought Thomas. How can we all be one with the idea of Jesus going to a cross? This will destroy all the faith people have had in Jesus.

Jesus continued:

> "Father, I want those you have given me to be with me where I am.... I made your name known to them and will continue to make it known, so that the love you have loved me with may be in them and I may be in them" (verses 24-26).

John looked directly into Jesus' face: We do love you, Jesus. Oh, how we love you. I love you more than any of the others. Please don't let us down.

* * *

"It is time to marshal the horses of providence that Zechariah saw in his vision," pronounced Michael.

"The horses being God's providential strategy for keeping his agenda on course," added Gabriel.

"Yes. We know God has often marshaled his horses of providence to keep his sovereign agenda on track. But we are going to need more angels to marshal the horses than ever before. God has allowed Satan, through his deputy Pan and all the other imps, to flood the atmosphere with darkness and confusion to manipulate the people against Jesus. Yes. Keep in mind God has allowed this, a horse of his planning. Pan has it all planned out how to crucify Jesus. And he is so focused on the single goal of destroying Jesus he is totally blind to the consequences—just what we want."

"God is going to allow Pan to carry out his purpose, but here is the catch: God is assigning us the responsibility to place controls on Pan's actions to show how the Passover and the Tamid (the daily sacrifice) foreshadow the crucifixion.

"We will control the timing of events for Jesus to be crucified on Passover day and control other details to show he is the final Passover Lamb. We will also see to it that many details of the crucifixion happen at the same time as corresponding aspects of the Tamid sacrifice which will be happening in the Temple. This will show how the Tamid has been foreshadowing the crucifixion. All of this will show that Jesus is the final, atoning sacrifice represented in the lamb sacrifices. Also, we will control other events to fulfill other foreshadowing of Jesus in the scriptures. We will not be making the events happen of course. That is the devil's dirty work. But we can control the timing."

"Wow," said Gabriel. "This is going to be fascinating."

"And we will make it obvious that Jesus regains in the Garden what Adam lost in the Garden," continued Michael. "People with insight will see that the animal sacrifices have only been tokens of the atonement provided in him. Christ's blood is the only blood precious enough to atone for the whole human race. This intelligence is top secret, the most highly classified intel ever. The page on which it was written in the Book of Truth was locked until now.[36]

"We don't dare let Satan and his demons know," asserted Gabriel."

"Yes. But they are all so focused on their evil mission that they wouldn't understand now, even if we told them. We will operate in full view of all. God is allowing the imps' single-minded purpose to blackout their minds to the consequences. The Lord certainly does not create evil. But when it is important to his horse-strategy, he will help those who are bent on doing evil to follow through by darkening their understanding of consequences."

"Like he did with Pharaoh," inserted Gabriel.

"Yes. Pharaoh was so bent on getting the Israelites back to Egypt that the danger of the walled waters of the Red Sea collapsing never dawned on him. He just went charging into the space between the walls of water," added Michael.

"Yes, real flesh-and-blood horses were involved in that strategy," laughed Gabriel.

"Indeed. God's horse of providential strategy made the flesh-and-blood horses of Pharaoh's army charge the Egyptians directly

---

[36] Daniel 10:21

into their destruction," Michael continued. "We have a distinct advantage over Satan in the planning of strategy. The Spirit of God will direct every angel in every detail of manipulating the evil plans of the enemy. We don't have to assign work to any. The Spirit will be in touch with all of us directly. We will each be keenly aware of his presence and direction at all times. And I will acknowledge to all the angels each scheduled fulfillment as it happens so we can each rejoice in the salvation being provided."

* * *

Coming to the Garden of Gethsemane with the disciples following him, Jesus admonished,

> "Pray that you may not fall into temptation." Then he withdrew from them about a stone's throw, knelt down, and began to pray, "Father, if you are willing, take this cup away from me—nevertheless, not my will, but yours, be done" (Luke 22:40-42).

* * *

"Number one fulfillment is in place," pronounced Michael. "Jesus has submitted to the will of the Father so he is set to fulfill the promise of redemption: 'he will bruise your head.'[37] Jesus is the second Adam. Adam was the man from the dust. Jesus is the man from heaven who is set to redeem what the man from the dust lost."[38]

* * *

Gabriel appeared to Jesus to strengthen him. He must have whispered, "You have just positioned yourself in this garden to gain

---

[37] Genesis 3:15
[39] See Mishnah, Tamid, 1, 2; Mishnah, Yoma, 1, 8, 2,3

Foresight

what Adam lost in his garden through rebellion against God's will. We angels will strengthen you to go obediently to the cross to redeem Adam's race from the curse he brought on his race."

The assault was under way. Jewish officials with their guards, Roman soldiers, and Malchus, the high priest's servant came with lanterns, torches, and weapons.

Jesus went directly to them. "Whom are you seeking?"

"Jesus of Nazareth."

"I am," Jesus said.

Instantly the whole crowd fell backward to the ground.

When they arose, Jesus asked them again, "Whom are you seeking?"

"Jesus of Nazareth."

"I told you I am. Let these who are with me go."

Peter's sword cut through the air. Malchus' severed ear went flying.

Instantly, before anyone could react, Jesus reached out and touched the wound and a new ear appeared.

Everyone, friends and foes alike, stood stunned. Not a person moved or spoke. Jesus had just named himself, "I am," appropriating God's name. And he had instantly replaced an ear in rebuke of his disciple's aggressive attack. The paralyzing impact on the militant crowd held them back from instantly arresting or killing Peter on the spot.

Jesus broke the spell, "Peter, put your sword away. Am I not to drink the cup the Father has given me?" (John 18:11).

Then the guards seized Jesus and led him away to the high priest's house, and the high priest said to him:

"I command you by the living God, tell us if you are the Christ, the Son of God."

> Jesus said to him, "You have said so. But I tell you, from now on you will see the Son of Man seated at the right hand of Power and coming on the clouds of heaven."
>
> Then the high priest tore his robes and said, "He has uttered blasphemy. What further witnesses do we need? You have now heard his blasphemy. What is your judgment?" They answered, "He deserves death" (Matthew 26:63-66).

* * *

"Number two fulfillment," pronounced Michael. "The high priest and the scribes and elders have just pronounced that Jesus deserves death. And the cock has crowed just now signaling the priests to make the first preparations in the temple to offer the Tamid (daily sacrifice) for sin. Just now the priests are casting lots in the temple to see who will remove the ashes from yesterday's sacrifice, who will slaughter the daily sacrifice, who will throw the blood onto the brazen altar, and other duties.[39]

"Yes, we have it documented that the first preparations for Jesus' sacrifice—which the Tamid clearly foreshadows—have just been made. And the first preparations for today's Tamid sacrifice have just been made at this approximate time."

* * *

> Then the whole company of them arose and brought him before Pilate. And they began to accuse him, saying, "We found this man misleading our nation and forbidding us to give tribute to Caesar, and saying that he himself is Christ, a king."
>
> And Pilate asked him, "Are you the King of the Jews?"

---

[39] See Mishnah, Tamid, 1, 2; Mishnah, Yoma, 1, 8, 2,3

Foresight

> And he answered him, "You have said so."
> Then Pilate said to the chief priests and the crowds, "I find no guilt in this man."
> But they were urgent, saying, "He stirs up the people, teaching throughout all Judea, from Galilee even to this place" (Luke 23:1-5).

Pilate didn't want to be responsible for judging Jesus so he sent him to Herod, making the excuse that he was from Herod's district. But Herod didn't want any more blood on his hands either. He had already killed enough people, including John the Baptist, to have a seriously troubled conscience. So Herod sent Jesus back to Pilate.

> Pilate then called together the chief priests and the rulers and the people, and said to them, "You brought me this man as one who was misleading the people. And after examining him before you, behold, I did not find this man guilty of any of your charges against him. Neither did Herod, for he sent him back to us. Look, nothing deserving death has been done by him. I will therefore punish and release him" (Luke 23:13-16).
> But they all cried out together, "Away with this man, and release to us Barabbas"—a man who had been thrown into prison for an insurrection started in the city and for murder. Pilate addressed them once more, desiring to release Jesus, but they kept shouting, "Crucify, crucify him."
> A third time he said to them, "Why? What evil has he done? I have found in him no guilt deserving death. I will therefore punish and release him" (Luke 23:18-22).

* * *

"Number three fulfillment has been made," cried Michael with extra exuberance in his voice. "It is just after dawn. The Levite on the pinnacle of the Temple has just seen the sun come up and shouted

'Barkai!' meaning, 'morning has arrived.'[40] This has prompted the priest in the temple to immediately make the final check of the Tamid lamb for any blemish.[41] He has pronounced the lamb to be without blemish. And Pilate has now made his third declaration that Jesus is without any blemish of guilt. The fulfillment of the foreshadowing continues."

* * *

Finally, Pilate gave in. He released the one who had been convicted of insurrection and murder. But he delivered Jesus over to the Jews' demands.

> So they took Jesus, and he went out, bearing his own cross, to the place called The Place of a Skull, which in Aramaic is called Golgotha.[42]
> They offered him wine to drink, mixed with gall, but when he tasted it, he would not drink it (Matthew 27:34-35).

* * *

"Number four, Jesus the only Son of God, the promised one, has carried his wooden cross up the hill to his sacrifice. Isaac, the son of promise of Abraham, carried the wood up a mountain to his sacrifice. This happened in this same region of mountains called the Mountains of Moriah. The foreshadowing continues.

"We also have number five fulfillment," added Michael. "They just offered Jesus wine with a narcotic to drink. He refused it and its numbing effects so as not to save himself from any of the agony his

---

[40] Mishnah Tamid 3:2
[41] Mishnah Tamid 3:2-4

[42] John 19:16-17

Foresight

Father chose for him to endure. But the drink was offered immediately preceding their acts to kill him. The Tamid lamb in the temple has been given a drink at this approximate time from a golden cup immediately preceding the priest's act to kill it."[43]

* * *

They crucified Jesus at the third hour (9:00 a.m.) and nailed a placard on the cross that read, "The King of the Jews." They also crucified two robbers with him, one on his right and one on his left.

* * *

"We have the big number six fulfillment. Jesus has been nailed to the cross at the third hour, 9:00 a.m. The morning Tamid lamb has also been slain this morning sometime after dawn."

* * *

At the sixth hour (12:00 p.m.) it suddenly became dark over the whole land until the ninth hour (3:00 p.m.).

> Jesus cried with a loud voice, "Eloi, Eloi, lema sabachthani?" which means, "My God, my God, why have you forsaken me?"
> And some of the bystanders hearing it said, "Behold, he is calling Elijah." And someone ran and filled a sponge with sour wine, put it on a reed and gave it to him to drink, saying, "Wait, and let us see whether Elijah will come to take him down."
> And Jesus uttered a loud cry and breathed his last. And the curtain of the temple was torn in two, from top to bottom. And when the centurion, who stood facing him, saw that in this way he breathed

---

[43] Mishnah Tamid 3:4

> his last, he said, "Truly this man was the Son of God" (Mark 15:33-39).
>
> When Jesus had received the sour wine, he said, "It is finished," and he bowed his head and gave up his spirit (John 19:30).

* * *

Michael drew in a big breath. "Jesus has just died. This has happened at the ninth hour, 3:00 p.m. And the evening Tamid lamb has just been offered at this time.[44] It is very significant that Jesus has been on the cross between the morning and afternoon sacrifices of the Tamid. Yes. Jesus continues to fulfill what the Tamid foreshadowed. His sacrifice fulfills the total picture of the Tamid.

"I am also recognizing number eight. Jesus just drank the wine (free of narcotics). He drank the sour wine, the cheaper wine of the common people to signify he was offering his life for everyone. In doing this, he drank the fourth cup of the traditional Passover meal, the Cup of Acceptance,[45] the one he avoided in his Passover meal with the disciples. This cup signified his acceptance of his Father's contract with him to provide a sin offering for all people. It alludes to the cup he referenced in the garden which he was willing to accept.

"However, Jesus also drank of the significance of the other three cups in offering himself on the cross as a sin offering," continued Michael. "He drank the Cup of Sanctification:[46]

> Jesus also suffered outside the gate in order to sanctify the people through his own blood (Hebrews 13:12).

---

[44] Josephus, *Antiquities of the Jews* 14:4.3 "Priests were not at all hindered from their sacred ministrations by their fear during this siege, but did still twice a-day, in the morning and about the ninth hour, offer their sacrifices on the altar; nor did they omit those sacrifices."

[45] Michal E. Hunt, *Jesus and the Mystery of the Tamid Sacrifice* (Thomas Nelson Publishers for Ignatius Press) Loc 2885

[46] Moishe Rosen, *Christ in the Passover* (Moody Publishers, Chicago) 126

Foresight

"He drank the Cup of Forgiveness by becoming the sin offering to provide justification for forgiveness:[47]

> For one will scarcely die for a righteous person—though perhaps for a good person one would dare even to die (Romans 5:7). In him we have redemption, the forgiveness of sins (Colossians 1:14).

"He drank the Cup of Redemption:[48]

> for all have sinned and fall short of the glory of God, and are justified by his grace as a gift, through the redemption that is in Christ Jesus (Romans 3:24).

"From now on Jesus' followers will drink only the cup of the Lord's Supper. It signifies acceptance of all four cups. Jesus said, 'This cup is the new covenant in my blood' (1Corinthians 11:25). Like a bride drinking the cup of her husband's proposal, it fully embraces the terms of the covenant.

"Accordingly, all should remember," Gabriel interjected:

> "For if we go on sinning deliberately after receiving the knowledge of the truth, there no longer remains a sacrifice for sins" (Hebrews 10:28).

"The covenant binds one to doing God's will and receiving deliverance from ongoing, deliberate sinning. Jesus did not provide a sacrifice to cover ongoing, deliberate sinning."

* * *

And the curtain of the temple was torn in two, from top to bottom. And when the centurion, who stood facing him, saw that in

---

[47] Michal E. Hunt, *Jesus and the Mystery of the Tamid Sacrifice* (Thomas Nelson Publishers for Ignatius Press) Loc 2885

[48] Moishe Rosen, *Christ in the Passover* (Moody Publishers, Chicago) 139
Michal E. Hunt, *Jesus and the Mystery of the Tamid Sacrifice* (Thomas Nelson Publishers for Ignatius Press) Loc 2885

World Crisis

* * *

"Number nine," pronounced Gabriel. "This is super huge. The thirty-foot-high curtain as thick as a man's hand which has separated the common people from direct access to God in the temple has been torn from top to bottom. Only God could have done this. Now people don't have to come through a priest to get forgiveness for sins. This is huge. Huge. Huge."

"There are other fulfillments," added Michael. "Jesus cried out in his most intense moment the exact words of Psalm 22:

"We will count this as number ten. And the same Psalm says,

"The soldiers cast lots for Jesus' garment. Clearly, this Psalm had foresight of these happenings in the crucifixion we just witnessed. This is number eleven."

"What about Isaiah 53?" asked Gabriel:

He was despised and rejected by men, a man of sorrows and acquainted with grief; and as one from whom men hide their faces he was despised, and we esteemed him not.

Surely he has borne our griefs and carried our sorrows; yet we esteemed him stricken, smitten by God, and afflicted.

But he was pierced for our transgressions; he was crushed for our iniquities; upon him was the chastisement that brought us peace, and with his wounds we are healed.

All we like sheep have gone astray; we have turned—everyone—to his own way; and the Lord has laid on him the iniquity of us all.

Foresight

> He was oppressed, and he was afflicted, yet he opened not his mouth; like a lamb that is led to the slaughter, and like a sheep that before its shearers is silent, so he opened not his mouth (Isaiah 53:4-7).

Michael interjected, "This is number twelve. Jesus has fulfilled all the foreshadowing of the crucifixion in the Old Testament."

Chapter 24

Resurrection and Ascension

Pan thrust his hands into the air. "Did you hear that? Jesus cried out, 'My God, My God, why have you forsaken me? Oh. And now he just said, 'It is finished' and died. This is even more than we could have hoped for. Jesus' plan to draw all people to himself has so utterly failed that the Father has forsaken him. We will soon have him in the grave with a big stone rolled in front of it. The Roman guards will make sure no one steals his body and proclaims that he rose from the dead. We have conquered the Lord God. Now we are in place to usurp authority over the universe."

"Congratulations to me," shouted Satan. "My strategy has worked. Now all you imps who are weak in your support of me had better come around. I, the great master strategist, have defeated God."

"How dare you! screamed Pan. "I was the one who planned the assault and directed it from start to finish. I will not let you take credit for this."

"Calm down there now, dear Pan. We are all evil spirits, remember. As the spirit I am, I was directing you in all that you did.

Foresight

And I would not advise you to challenge me. I am the ruler of this world, you know. Nobody—I mean nobody—will bring me down!"

* * *

Instantly, a powerful voice sounded, "What did you say, O judged ruler?"

Satan trembled. His black face turned pale. His knees gave way and he dropped to the mire. Pan stumbled backward and also began to tremble. All the imps were shaking and crying out in fear.

"You, O Satan, ruler of this world, are judged. You no longer have any grounds for insisting that people must go to Hades (Sheol) for their sin. Lazarus, who ate the crumbs from the rich man's table, and all saints who have died up until now are released from Hades. The robber on the cross who believed in me and all my followers from now on will never go to Hades. They will go to be with their Maker in heaven. My blood has been applied to set them free from death. You are disarmed of the accusations against those who believe in me. You are stripped of the prosecutor role you have usurped. You certainly have no claim on the souls of people.

"Look, 'The keys of Death and Hades'[49] are in my hands!"

* * *

The devils all closed their eyes to this sight. It was too much. An eerie silence permeated the atmosphere. When the imps finally opened their eyes, Jesus was gone.

Satan spoke with yet trembling voice. "I-I wan-nt you-u to reme-emb-eer that Jesus' body is still in the grave. All is not lost. We can still act as though we have the keys. We can lie people into believing Jesus has accomplished nothing. We can keep on enslaving them

---

[49] Revelation 1:18

Resurrection and Ascension

through deceit and intimidation. And we will keep the priests focused on continuing to offer the Tamid every day as though nothing has happened."

"Well this fits you, Satan," declared Pan. "You are full of lies, like the lie you told when you took credit for my efforts. As Jesus said, 'You speak out of your own character, for you are a liar and the father of lies.'"[50]

"This does it, Pan. You are removed from your position of leading the campaign of confusion and darkness. You are right. I do operate on lies but speaking the truth of Jesus is a serious no-no. I will have to invent other strategies for use with other demons than you imps of the Greek Zeus religion. You all have messed up royally. Now Jesus has the upper hand over us."

Zeus bared his teeth through his ugly face, "You haven't seen anything yet. This darkness and confusion campaign is about to backfire on us in an even greater way."

"What are you blowing about, pitiful Zeus of failed Greek religion?"

"Wait and see. Wait and see."

* * *

The angels flew impatiently around the crystal glass sea. Who would the Father send to free Jesus from the tomb and when would he send him? Sunday's morning sun rose over the horizon. The rays lit the space around the tomb and reflected off of the stone blocking the doorway. "Go!" shouted the one sitting on the throne, as he pointed to the most shining angel of all.

* * *

---

[50] See John 8:44

Foresight

The angel, normally transparent to the human eye, became opaque. His plunge to the earth coincided with a huge seismic shift and a great earthquake. The atmosphere flamed around him. His clothing, unfazed by the flame, was white as snow. The guards trembled in fear before him until all their strength was gone. Then they collapsed on the earth and were as still as death.

With one sweeping motion of his right arm, the angel rolled the stone away. Jesus emerged out of the grave clothes with a body not inhibited by physical elements. The clothes remained there, still formed in the shape of his body. He stepped triumphantly out of the clothes and the tomb. The angel entered the tomb, sat down, became transparent again, and waited.

Mary Magdalene, Mary, the mother of James, and Salome were on their way to the tomb carrying spices to anoint the body. Mary Magdalene suddenly stopped and looked at the others, "Who will roll the stone away for us?"

"I don't know," said Salome.

The other Mary said, "I am afraid to ask the guards. I understand the stone is sealed." They kept on walking.

They rounded the last curve in the path. "The stone is rolled away!" cried Mary Magdalene. "Oh no! Someone has carried him away."

Cautiously, they entered the tomb. They stared at the blank cold walls of stone with their backs turned to the angel. Suddenly, the angel became opaque again. His brightness lit up the stone cavity. The women spun around:

> But the angel said to the women, "Do not be afraid, for I know that you seek Jesus who was crucified. He is not here, for he has risen, as he said. Come, see the place where he lay. Then go quickly and tell his disciples that he has risen from the dead, and behold, he is going before you to Galilee; there you will see him. See, I have told you."

Resurrection and Ascension

So they departed quickly from the tomb with fear and great joy, and ran to tell his disciples.

And behold, Jesus met them and said, "Greetings." And they came up and took hold of his feet and worshiped him. Then Jesus said to them, "Do not be afraid; go and tell my brothers to go to Galilee, and there they will see me" (Matthew 28:6-10).

~

The disciples came together in Jerusalem to discuss the reports of Jesus rising. Suddenly Jesus stood in their presence and proclaimed,

"Peace to you." But they were startled and frightened and thought they saw a spirit. And he said to them, "Why are you troubled, and why do doubts arise in your hearts? See my hands and my feet, that it is I myself. Touch me, and see. For a spirit does not have flesh and bones as you see that I have" (Luke 24:36-39).

"Have you anything here to eat?"

They gave him a piece of broiled fish, and he took it and ate before them. Then he said to them, "These are my words that I spoke to you while I was still with you, that everything written about me in the Law of Moses and the Prophets and the Psalms must be fulfilled."

Then he opened their minds to understand the Scriptures, and said to them, "Thus it is written, that the Christ should suffer and on the third day rise from the dead, and that repentance for the forgiveness of sins should be proclaimed in his name to all nations, beginning from Jerusalem. You are witnesses of these things. And behold, I am sending the promise of my Father upon you. But stay in the city until you are clothed with power from on high" (Luke 24:41-49).

Then he led them to Bethany, blessing them with uplifted hands. Suddenly, gravity released him and he ascended into heaven. All the disciples bowed and worshiped and then returned to Jerusalem full of

Foresight

bountiful joy. There they continued to worship.

Chapter 25

Holy Spirit Baptism

The disciples and other followers of Jesus were hidden away in the upper room. Peter arose. "I am so unworthy to have the forgiveness of Christ, but I fully accept it. I want to wash the feet of all you disciples as Jesus taught us to do by his example. You will hear no more talk from me about who is the greatest."

"I will let you do this, Peter," replied Andrew as Peter came to him, "not because I am deserving but because I want to be a part of your submission to Christ."

The others all nodded the same sentiment. Peter approached John where he was seated. "My heart has been envious of you, John. I am so sorry." Tears flowed down John's cheeks as he stood up and hugged Peter.

Bartholomew was ready with his confession as Peter approached him. "Peter, I am sorry for the standoffish attitude I have had toward you. I was jealous of your close relationship with Jesus. When Jesus blessed you for confessing that he was the Christ, the Son of the

Foresight

Living God, I was thinking of saying the same thing, but you beat me to it. I was livid, because you got the credit. I am so sorry."

Tears gathered in Peter's eyes. "We are both on the same level before God, Bartholomew. God bless you."

"I have prepared the Lord's supper for us," said John softly with a twinkle in his eye. "We will no longer keep the traditional Passover, for the final Passover was fulfilled and finished in Christ's death on the cross. He was the ultimate sacrifice and the Lamb of all lambs. We will continue to remind ourselves of our covenant in Christ's blood, our covenant with our Savior. We will do this with the cup of the Lord's Supper and in the process enhance our fellowship with Jesus."

"In this new covenant, the *stone-cut-from-a-mountain* (the kingdom of God) is now about to be inaugurated *in* society. The kingdom operated from a distance in the old covenant. We are about to be 'clothed with power from on high'"[51] as Jesus promised. The Holy Spirit will be *in* us (the church) instead of just *with* us, or *upon* us. And in this occupancy, he will bring the kingdom of God to bear *in* society instead of just having it operate from a distance. Remember. Jesus promised the Helper who is the Holy Spirit:

> "I will ask the Father, and he will give you another Helper, to be with you forever, even the Spirit of truth, whom the world cannot receive, because it neither sees him nor knows him. You know him, for he dwells *with* you and will be *in* you" (John 14:16).

The Holy Spirit will be in us. And he will bring the kingdom into society through his rule from the throne of our hearts. God's whole operation will be different from his Old Testament operation." We thought the kingdom of Israel was *the stone-cut-from-a-mountain,* but I now see that this kingdom is not the earthly kingdom of Israel. It is a spiritual kingdom destined to rule the earth through changed

---

[51] Luke 24:49

Holy Spirit Baptism

hearts and free it from its self-centered corruption. Perhaps earthly kingdoms will eventually be obsolete.

The atmosphere of forgiveness and love permeated every heart. All seventy souls were weeping and smiling their spirit of humility and acceptance of each other. This attitude continued in prayer and meditation as they waited to be clothed with the power Jesus had promised. For weeks they waited, hidden away from those who wanted to stomp all faith in Jesus from the land.

~

They all heard it on the day of Pentecost. It sounded like a mighty rushing wind swirling within the entire house where they were sitting. Fire-like tongues appeared on everyone. At the same instant, all were filled with the Holy Spirit who gave them words to speak in other tongues. Since it was Pentecost, devout Jews from many nations of different languages were at Jerusalem for the feast.

When they heard the mighty, rushing wind sound, they all rushed to the scene and found the disciples preaching. To their utter bewilderment, each one was hearing them speak in his own language. Then, as they heard of the mighty works of God in this way, they said to one another, "What does this mean?"

But others mocking said, "They are filled with new wine."

All the speakers grew silent except Peter. He raised his voice and spoke with mighty conviction (Acts 2):

> "Men of Judea and all who dwell in Jerusalem, let this be known to you, and give ear to my words. For these people are not drunk, as you suppose, since it is only the third hour of the day. But this is what was uttered through the prophet Joel,
>
> "'And in the last days it shall be, God declares,
> that I will pour out my Spirit on all flesh, and your sons and your daughters shall prophesy, and your young men shall see visions, and your old men shall dream dreams; even on my male servants and

Foresight

> female servants in those days I will pour out my Spirit, and they shall prophesy'" (verses 14-18).

"Listen to this!" exclaimed Ariyah to Elisav. "We can be in touch with God personally like the other women we see being baptized with the Holy Spirit. We can have understanding of God's word from this relationship and teach others."

Elisav raised her hands and looked upward, "Well even now I spiritually sense the Spirit of God filling me. We can know God's will as the Spirit illuminates God's word to us."

"I am aware of the same; the Spirit fills me also. As we hear the apostles speak, the Spirit confirms they are speaking the truth."

"I believe this means we can have the Spirit's daily guidance. He will show us how to serve God," declared Elisav.

Peter continued, quoting Joel the prophet:

> "And I will show wonders in the heavens above and signs on the earth below, blood, and fire, and vapor of smoke; the sun shall be turned to darkness and the moon to blood, before the day of the Lord comes, the great and magnificent day. And it shall come to pass that everyone who calls upon the name of the Lord shall be saved" (verses 19-21).

Stephen reached over and put his hand on Nicanor's shoulder, "Obviously, God is really going to be shaking the world with the outpouring of the Holy Spirit in light of these metaphors. How refreshing to know that righteousness is going to prevail!"

"You don't think this means that the Spirit is going to bring physical blood, fire, and smoke?" questioned Nicanor.

"Well, Peter just said this is what Joel prophesied about— blood, and fire, and vapor of smoke with the sun being turned to darkness and the moon to blood. And obviously, these things are not literally happening, so this manner of speaking is a picturesque way of speaking about spiritual truths."

Holy Spirit Baptism

Stephen raised his hand to his chin and looked thoughtfully into the distance. "Human words cannot always give precise definitions to God's spiritual activity. But the phenomenon of the natural world often can give us a picture of spiritual dynamics. Therefore, God speaks in these terms."

Nicanor replied, "Yes, the vapor of smoke, the sun becoming dark, and the moon becoming blood must allude symbolically to the mighty, earthshaking impact the gospel is having and will continue to have. However, the blood may allude to the blood of Jesus shed for us. And the sun becoming dark may allude to the darkness that came at noon when Jesus was on the cross."

Steven added, "I believe the earth shaking is going to have a profoundly spiritual impact on us. The Holy Spirit will set our hearts aflame with his *love*, fill our lives with purpose and *hope*, and give us *faith* to expect a great awakening. This will make us spiritual instead of worldly, conditioning us to live in the presence and fellowship of the Spirit,[52] much like Adam and Eve did before they fell. Through this fellowship, God's power can surge through us to convict the world of sin, righteousness, and judgment."[53]

Nicanor looked at his friend in amazement, "I believe the spirit of prophecy is on you. You are filled with the Holy Spirit."

Peter's voice continued to ring out loud and clear, being heard in all the different native languages of the people present:

> "Men of Israel, hear these words, Jesus of Nazareth, a man attested to you by God with mighty works and wonders and signs that God did through him in your midst, as you yourselves know—this Jesus, delivered up according to the definite plan and foreknowledge of God, you crucified and killed by the hands of lawless men. God raised him up" (verses 22-24).
>
> "This Jesus God raised up, and of that we all are witnesses. Being

---

[52] 2 Corinthians 13:14
[53] John 16:18

Foresight

therefore exalted at the right hand of God, and having received from the Father the promise of the Holy Spirit, he has poured out this that you yourselves are seeing and hearing" (verses 32-33).

"Let all the house of Israel therefore know for certain that God has made him both Lord and Christ, this Jesus whom you crucified" (verse 36).

When the people heard this, they were convicted by the Holy Spirit and asked:

"Brothers, what shall we do?" (verse 37).

And Peter said to them, "Repent and be baptized every one of you in the name of Jesus Christ for the forgiveness of your sins, and you will receive the gift of the Holy Spirit. For the promise is for you and for your children and for all who are far off, everyone whom the Lord our God calls to himself" (verses 38-39).

Martha declared to Mary, "The Holy Spirit is moving on all present. A great spiritual deluge is flooding the atmosphere. I doubt that the world has ever experienced such spiritual impact."

Mary hugged her sister. "I feel a great warmth of the Spirit spreading throughout Jerusalem and beyond," she said. "What marvels we are yet to see with our eyes—what Joel only saw in a prophetic vision. The Holy Spirit is anointing his people with great faith expectancy. He is calling them to *identify with Christ's operation to save the lost and conquer the kingdom of the world.*"

~

Saul of Tarsus pounded the desk of the high priest, "Why are we allowing this Jesus heresy to spread? We must stop it now before it gets completely out of hand."

"What do you suggest that we do, angry soul?"

"Give me letters of authority to go to the synagogues in Damascus and bind any of this Way and bring them back here for judgment."

Holy Spirit Baptism

The high priest pulled a parchment from the shelf behind him and quickly scribbled, "Be it known to all that Saul of Tarsus has authority to bind any followers of Jesus and take them to the council in Jerusalem to be judged for spreading heresy."

He signed the note and stamped it with his stamp. "Here is your authorization. And from now on, be a little more respectful of the priesthood."

"I will when you get off your lazy seat and get moving against the doctrines that are assaulting Almighty God and our cherished traditions."

The high priest rose from behind the desk and thrust his finger in Saul's face—where Saul's face had been—and yelled, "I will teach you Saul "

But Saul was on his way out the door. "Let's go men!" he shouted tersely to his disciples. "We will destroy them. We will conquer them. We will bind up these people with their doctrines and false reports that Jesus rose from the dead." He fairly snorted like a mad bull, "We will wipe this movement from the earth."

Young Saul charged ahead, his disciples struggling to keep up through the streets of Jerusalem and on to the road going north. In about nine miles they met an intersection where they turned east for about twenty-three miles, crossing the Jordan River to the Way of the Plain where they turned north. They trekked through the Jordan Valley on this road at a brisk pace each day and slept along the road at night for several days. Eventually the road curved northeast until it brought them to the road to Damascus which turned them more directly north again.

Now, nearing Damascus:

Suddenly a light from heaven shone around him. And falling to the ground, he heard a voice saying to him, "Saul, Saul, why are you persecuting me?" And he said, "Who are you, Lord?" And he said, "I

Foresight

Those who were traveling with Saul were stunned into silence. They heard the voice but saw no one. Saul rose from the ground, only to realize he was blind. He could see nothing. His men had to lead him by the hand into Damascus. There for three days he could not see and refused to eat or drink anything.

A Christ-follower named Ananias was in prayer:

"Lord said to him in a vision, 'Ananias.' And he said, 'Here I am, Lord.'" And the Lord said to him, "Rise and go to the street called Straight, and at the house of Judas look for a man of Tarsus named Saul, for behold, he is praying" (Acts 9:10-11).

What could this mean? pondered Ananias. Is the man who has been crazy with hatred for us praying to Jesus? Could he actually be looking for me to instruct him as I understood the Lord to tell me in my vision? I am a little apprehensive, but I will go to him as the Lord has instructed me.

He immediately got ready and set out for Judas' house. There he met Saul and said to him, "Brother Saul, the Lord Jesus who appeared to you on the road by which you came has sent me so that you may regain your sight and be filled with the Holy Spirit."

Immediately, he regained his sight as the Holy Spirit filled him. Overjoyed, he rose and was baptized. Then he ate and was strengthened.

~

Peter was residing with Simon the tanner in his house at Joppa by the Mediterranean Sea (Acts 10). About noon, he went up on the housetop to pray. The physical exertion of his fervency in prayer made him hungry. In this state he fell into a trance. The heavens opened with something like a large sheet being let down by its four corners. In it were all kinds of animals, reptiles, and birds. Then a voice rang out:

Holy Spirit Baptism

"Rise, Peter; kill and eat." But Peter said, "By no means, Lord; for I have never eaten anything that is common or unclean." And the voice came to him again a second time, "What God has made clean, do not call common" (verses 13-15).

This happened three times.

~

Peter was in shock as he trekked with the men who had come to invite him to the house of Cornelius, the Roman Centurion. I am overwhelmed with all that has been happening, he mused. First Jesus disappoints us all by submitting to the cross. Then in our despair he rises from the dead and our deep grief turns to cautious joy. Next, we Jews are filled with the Spirit and with hope for our nation. Now I am instructed to go to the Gentiles to share the gospel with them. Actually, this is good news because so many of my nation are rejecting Jesus. But oh, what shocks and surprises!

"Welcome, Peter," said Cornelius when Peter arrived at his house.

"Good day, sir. I understood you would know my name. But now it is confirmed in my mind that the Lord has instructed you to call for me. What is this all about?"

"The other day, I was praying and suddenly a man in dazzling clothing stood before me. He told me that God had heard my prayers and that I should send for you, a man named Simon, also called Peter. Obviously, the Lord has something to say to us through you."

Peter began:

"Truly I understand that God shows no partiality, but in every nation anyone who fears him and does what is right is acceptable to him. As for the word that he sent to Israel, preaching good news of peace through Jesus Christ (he is Lord of all), you yourselves know what happened throughout all Judea, beginning from Galilee after the baptism that John proclaimed, how God anointed Jesus of Nazareth with the Holy Spirit and with power. He went about doing good and

Foresight

healing all who were oppressed by the devil, for God was with him. And we are witnesses of all that he did both in the country of the Jews and in Jerusalem.

"They put him to death by hanging him on a tree, but God raised him on the third day and made him to appear, not to all the people but to us who had been chosen by God as witnesses, who ate and drank with him after he rose from the dead. And he commanded us to preach to the people and to testify that he is the one appointed by God to be judge of the living and the dead. To him all the prophet's bear witness that everyone who believes in him receives forgiveness of sins through his name" (verses 34-43).

Suddenly the Holy Spirit fell on all the Gentiles present. The Jews who had come with Peter were awestruck. They never expected the Holy Spirit to be poured out on Gentiles. They, like Peter, had understood that the Spirit was only for the circumcised, the Jews. The Gentiles even began praising God in the various native tongues of listeners present. Yet the speakers had never learned the languages they were speaking.

Then Peter declared, "Can anyone withhold water for baptizing these people, who have received the Holy Spirit just as we have?" And he commanded them to be baptized in the name of Jesus Christ. Then they asked him to remain for some days (verses 47-48).

* * *

The hapless devil and his miserable imps watched in horror and finally got themselves together enough to have a meeting. "What will we do, Satan?" lamented Ares. "The kingdom of God is crushing us."

"You should be asking, the way you and Pan messed up by crucifying Jesus. That allowed Jesus to break the claim we had on souls "by canceling the record of debt that stood against them with

Holy Spirit Baptism

its legal demands."[54]

"Jesus nailed this record that gave us grounds to accuse the servants of God before his throne to the cross. But then God wasn't satisfied until he disarmed us rulers and authorities and put us to open shame, by triumphing over us in Jesus."[55]

"You're getting to be quite the preacher for Jesus," taunted Ares.

"That does it, Ares. Away with you! Demons, come and take Ares and Pan away. Banish them from my presence," demanded Satan.

But no imp made a move. They only glared at the one who proclaimed himself to be their king. Pan shouted, "We all know that you were as much for the scheme to crucify Jesus as any of us. How dare you?"

"Well now, I don't want to have mutiny here," confessed the wicked one.

The demons drew closer, snarling ever louder.

"Ok. Ok. I get it. You want to forget our past. And really, this is a good idea, because we must look to the future."

"We have done some good, like getting Stephen stoned. That was good, I guess—maybe not. Saul turned to Jesus as a result."

Jupiter lifted his dirty chin, "My brilliance engineered that while the rest of you imps of Greek religion were moping about, all depressed about Jesus rising from the dead. When Stephen was exalting Jesus, I stirred up just the right persons to start grinding their teeth and shouting, 'Stone this guy!' Immediately, others followed suit. They charged at Stephen, threw him out of town, and stoned him."

"Good going, Jupiter!" exclaimed Satan. "This confirms to me that we need to appoint you, Juno, Minerva, Neptune, Venus, Mars, Apollo, and Diana who have been working behind the scenes to come to the forefront of our fight. Yes, we need to make the others aware

---

[54] See Colossians 2:14
[55] See Colossians 2:13-15

Foresight

that by my direction you have been inspiring the Romans to revise the old Greek religion. This had to be a highly classified operation to keep the Greeks from being upset. So don't anyone be offended that you were not informed."

"Now Jupiter, who is the most vulnerable and the best candidate for us to possess?" asked Satan.

"I suggest we start with King Herod Agrippa I. He is the son of Herod Antipas who killed John the Baptist and the grandson of Herod the Great. He is an extremely proud egotist, so he is very vulnerable. And of course, he is ruler over Judea and Jerusalem. We can create havoc through him for the believers of the new Way, right there in their central operation in Jerusalem."

"I am counting on you," declared Satan.

* * *

Agrippa spoke to his counselors, "What can we do to make the irascible Jews happy? They can make life miserable for us when they are unhappy."

Ram spoke up, "I have the politically-expedient solution in mind, but it will not be considered righteous."

"Well, don't you know by now we do what is politically expedient? Forget the morality aspect. We cannot be much worse sinners than the Jews anyway. They crucified Jesus just because they were jealous of him."

"Then go arrest James the son of Zebedee and kill him. The Jews will love you for it. Your judgment on James will enable them to rationalize that your deed was an act of God. It will confirm what they want to believe: God wants the Jesus movement destroyed."

"Okay, Ram. You know how to get the job done," Agrippa commissioned.

Holy Spirit Baptism

~

Peter awoke from his sound sleep, feeling the jolt on his side. There stood the Angel who had just struck him. Comprehension began to dawn. I am in Herod's prison chained between two guards. I think this angel just said, "Get up quickly. Dress yourself and put on your sandals." Oh wow. My chains just fell off. I will get dressed.

"Wrap your cloak around you and follow me."

"Okay, I will do so gladly."

Peter was thinking, we have just passed the first and the second prison guards. Now we are going through the iron gate of this prison right out into the city. Wow. The gate opened for us of its own accord.

"Where are we headed, angel?" Peter stared in shock. The angel had just vanished. Oh! This is not a vision like I was thinking.

Out loud he said, "Now I am sure that the Lord has sent his angel and rescued me from the hand of Herod and all those who want me dead. I sure wish James could have been delivered like this before Herod killed him. How sad it is to not have his exuberant presence with us anymore."

* * *

"I am so thrilled to see how the church has grown. The gospel spreads like wildfire," pronounced Gabriel.

"Or like leaven in flour," smiled Michael.

"Oh yes. Like Jesus would put it," observed Gabriel. "I have been thinking about the parable of the leaven ever since Jesus told it. Jesus said the woman hid the leaven in three measures of flour, right?"

"Yes."

"The flour symbolizes society, right?"

"That is the way I see it."

"All that is in the world, the three measures: the lust of the flesh,

Foresight

the lust of the eyes, and the pride....."[56]

"Oh yes. I see where you are going with this, Gabriel! The gospel leaven is hidden in the three -isms of the world for the purpose of leavening society. The gospel is the leaven turning people to Jesus even as wicked people still exist in it. This paves the way for the gospel to conquer the three -isms of the devil with faith, love, and hope in many lives as we have been observing."

"As I was saying, the gospel is spreading like wildfire or as you observed, it is spreading like leaven in the flour of society to pervade it with strong Christian influence. God's kingdom is not of this world. It is not intended to produce *political dominion*. But it is intended to build a prevailing Christian influence in the world. Peter took the gospel to the Gentiles in Caesarea. And the followers of Jesus scattered across the land after Stephen was stoned. They traveled as far as Phoenicia, Cyprus, and Antioch of Syria spreading the gospel."

"Yes, and the church at Jerusalem heard of the massive growth of the church at Antioch," inserted Gabriel.

"Indeed, they did. Then they sent Barnabas, a man full of the Holy Spirit, to encourage them. His lively exhortation was like fuel on the fire. The Holy Spirit poured out his love and anointing, producing teachers and prophets. They all were so full of the Holy Spirit they could not keep quiet. They spread the gospel with power and anointing."

"It was so amazing to see the devil and his bewildered imps running here and there trying to put a damper on things." said Gabriel. "But the more attacks they made, the faster the gospel spread."

"Oh yes!" replied Michael. "Saul started going by his other name, Paul. And the Holy Spirit called him and Barnabas at Antioch of Syria to go to the Gentiles with the Gospel. This developed into a mighty Holy Spirit-awakening among the Gentiles."

Gabriel raised his hands in an attitude of praise to the Lord, "Yes,

---

[56] 1 John 2:16 KJV

they went to Antioch of Pisidia where many Jews and Gentiles came to Christ. They came in spite of great opposition from unbelieving Jews. They preached the Word in Iconuim, Lystra, Derbe, and the surrounding country. Other missionary journeys took them farther west to Asia, which will come to be known as Turkey, and Greece."

Michael smiled broadly. "I had to send extra angels to join you in protecting and guiding the missionaries like Paul, Barnabas, and Silas. I had to do the same for John Mark and Luke as they ministered in Lystra, Ephesus, Troas, Galatia, Lystra, Thessalonica, Philippi, Berea, Corinth and many other places."

"Yes, we really got busy when Paul was stoned and left for dead in Lystra," said Gabriel, "We drove the stoners away and strengthened Paul to rise up and go on his way in full recovery. We had to work from many angles at Philippi when Paul and Silas were cast into prison. We also had to protect Paul and his companions in the storms at sea and the shipwreck at Malta on Paul's way to Rome.

"By the way, being in prison hasn't kept Paul from preaching the gospel. His letters have more potential to influence the world with gospel than all his awesome, in-person, foreign missionary preaching. His verve, sparkle, and anointing come through even in his letters," declared Gabriel.

"Yes, multitudes will be living witnesses of what Jesus has done for them as a result of his imprisonment. They have received the testimony of faith to their own salvation as will be expressed in John's future letter:

Whoever believes in the Son of God has the testimony in himself. Whoever does not believe God has made him a liar, because he has not believed in the testimony that God has borne concerning his Son (John 5:10).

And the Spirit testifies to them as Paul will declare:

The Spirit himself bears witness with our spirit that we are children of God (Romans 8:16).

Foresight

As this happens, those born into the family of God testify to others of their assurance of salvation. So the Gospel continues to spread like wildfire. We angels can expect to have more and more work as time goes on. And you know what, Michael, I believe the time is coming when earthly governmental kingdoms will become obsolete as God's kingdom advances its rule through changed hearts. Evidently this will lead to a new creation. We read in Paul's letter to the Romans that "the creation itself will be set free from its bondage to corruption" (Romans 8:21).

"Yes Gabriel, in the light of all that is happening, I am reminded of the Jerusalem without walls that one of our fellow angels told Zechariah would be built. Could the church that is developing be this Jerusalem, a spiritual Jerusalem?

"You are right, Michael. The church is the new Jerusalem and the people believing in Christ are the new temple. Each Christian is a temple in one sense, and in another sense, all the believers collectively are the temple. The present-day Jerusalem and the physical temple of today are becoming obsolete. As to whether there will be a future physical Jerusalem which plays a part in Christ *operation to save the lost and conquer the kingdom of the world*, this is something that has not been revealed to me."

Chapter 26

Apostle Paul and Aristarchus

Aristarchus sat in rapt attention before his close friend and mentor Paul who was under house arrest in the Praetorium of Caesar at Rome.

"Aristarchus, I will never be able to thank you enough for your faithfulness to me in all we have been through. In Ephesus many turned to the Lord and quit worshiping their god Artemis. As a result, Demetrius and the other craftsmen whose business depended on creating idols stirred up a huge mob against us. But you stood to the forefront to protect me from the brunt of the attack. This resulted in the angry crowd dragging you and Gaius before the town clerk.

"You have always been willing to lay your life on the line for me. You ministered to me when I was in prison for declaring the gospel—the mystery of Christ bringing salvation to all. You stood in the gap caused by my absence by keeping in touch with the churches. You continue to minister to my every need while I am under house arrest here in Rome. I thank you for being such a faithful friend."

"Think nothing of it, Brother Paul. I have great joy in being of service to you for Christ's sake. By the way, would you be interested in highlighting some of the basic truths of your epistles?"

"I will be glad to speak of building relationship with God and

Foresight

doing his will. Let's start by focusing on faith, love, and hope. I have expressed the importance of these dynamics in relation to each other in nine places in my epistles. And by the way, so has Peter in two places in his first epistle. [57] Besides this, I refer to faith, love, and hope in many other places in my epistles without mentioning all three in relation to each other.

"The most basic of all salvation-basics is that we are saved—born of the Spirit—through faith. People receive salvation through faith in Jesus, not by meriting it through works. However, with faith comes love, for the Holy Spirit pours out his love in our hearts when we are born of the Spirit. And the faith-love relationship then produces hope which enables us to prevail in doing exploits for God. Without godly hope we would not have the necessary incentive to prevail.

As we grow in the Lord, we need to *identify with Christ's operation to save the lost and conquer the kingdom of the world.* In doing so, we tend to want to do as I wrote to the Romans:

> Present your bodies as a living sacrifice, holy and acceptable to God, which is your spiritual worship. Do not be conformed to this world, but be transformed by the renewal of your mind, that by testing you may discern what is the will of God, what is good and acceptable and perfect. (Romans 12:1-2).

"This makes us 'dead to sin and alive to God' as I also wrote to the Romans (Romans 6:11). And in this dedication, the Holy Spirit who has birthed us spiritually, now can fill us. This transforms us by renewing our minds with God's thoughts and purposes. The infilling also pours out more of God's love in our hearts[58] and this love empowers our wills to do God's will. We no longer live just to pleasure our senses instead living in the joy of the Lord through

---

[57] Romans 5:1-5; 1 Corinthians 13:4 &13; Galatian 5:5-6; Ephesians 1:15-19; Colossians 1:3-6; 1 Thessalonians 1:2-4, 5:8-9; Hebrews 6:10-12;10:19-25;
[58] Romans 5:5

prayer, study of God's word, and fellowship with our Maker. Therefore, we are no longer "lovers of pleasure rather than of lovers of God" (2 Timothy 3:4). All of this is about being sanctified entirely according to what I wrote to the Thessalonians:

"Now may the God of peace himself sanctify you completely, and may your whole spirit and soul and body be kept blameless at the coming of our Lord Jesus Christ" (1 Thessalonians 5:23).

"This sanctification brings us into intimate fellowship of the Spirit, allowing him to dominate our senses and natural cravings. Without this, our bodily senses and cravings are dominant, driving us to live for what gratifies our senses, tending to make us lovers of sensory pleasure rather than lovers of God. We are either lovers of pleasure just living to gratify our senses in the physical world, or we are lovers of God, gratifying our spirits with the joy of the Lord as we develop spiritual sensitivity to his leadership.

Of course we all enjoy the physical world through our senses. But if we are lovers of God, we tend to be more oriented to the spiritual realm than to the physical realm. We learn that fellowshipping with God brings the joy of the Lord which far exceeds any pleasure or happiness received by serving our senses.

Paul continued, "The presence of the Spirit and the love he pours out in our hearts powerfully motivates us. This frees us from being dependent on law and a sense of duty to motivate us. God's love puts a love for his law in our hearts. In a sense, it writes the law on our hearts[59] so that doing God's will becomes our main desire.

"Feeding on the word of God helps write God's word on our hearts and maintains the renewal of our minds to keep inlign with God's thoughts and purposes. The Word keeps us looking to Jesus for strength and encouragement. He is the founder and perfecter of our faith."[60]

---

[59] Jeremiah 31:33
[60] See Hebrews 12:2

Foresight

Now with these spiritual developments, our hearts come in tune with the heart of God who desires to save the world. This further *identifies us with his operation to save the lost and conquer the kingdom of the world.* This will tend to give us a passion to pray for a great world-wide spiritual awakening to further this cause. When we pray together for this, our passion tends to increase until we are effectively interceding in prayer. The collective, fervent prayer-agreement is blended with God's will to move him to continue to free the creation from its bondage as I wrote to the Romans:

> For the creation waits with eager longing for the revealing of the sons of God. For the creation was subjected to futility, not willingly, but because of him who subjected it, in *hope* [21] that the creation itself will be set free from its bondage to corruption and obtain the freedom of the glory of the children of God (Romans 8:19-21).

And with this, prayer we are moved to witness for the Lord and show his *love* to our neighbors through whatever means we can. We do this in the *hope* of winning them to *faith* in the Lord—to the *hope* in the promises of God they will find in their new-creation relationship with God.

Aristarchus looked directly into Paul's eyes and remembered Paul's passion for his own people, "What about the Hebrews, the physical offspring of Abraham? What is God's plan for them?"

"I will give you my words from my epistle to the Romans:

> Has God rejected his people? By no means. For I myself am an Israelite, a descendant of Abraham, a member of the tribe of Benjamin. God has not rejected his people whom he foreknew. Do you not know what the Scripture says of Elijah, how he appeals to God against Israel? "Lord, they have killed your prophets, they have demolished your altars, and I alone am left, and they seek my life." But what is God's reply to him? "I have kept for myself seven thousand men who have not bowed the knee to Baal." So too at the present time there is a *remnant*, chosen by grace" (Romans 11:1-5).

"God has reserved a *remnant* among them with whom he can

Apostle Paul and Aristarchus

keep his *covenant*."

"Can you explain more to me about this *remnant*, Brother Paul?"

"Well, the branches of unbelieving Jews have been broken off of God's *covenant* olive tree—the tree that grew from the root of God's *covenants* with Abraham and David. The believing Gentiles, the wild olive branches, have been grafted into God's *covenant* tree (see Romans 11:17-23). But many Jews also believe in Jesus. They are the *remnant,* remaining in the tree, through which God is keeping his *covenant* with Abraham relative to his physical offspring. God said to Abraham,

> I will bless those who bless you, and him who dishonors you I will curse, and in you all the families of the earth shall be blessed (Genesis 12:3).
>
> And I will establish my *covenant* between me and you and your offspring after you throughout their generations for an everlasting *covenant*, to be God to you and to your offspring after you (Genesis 17:7).

"But these promises extend further than to just the physical offspring of Abraham. This is why the believing Gentiles have been grafted into the *covenant* tree."

Aristarchus shifted his gaze upward in thought. "Seems to me you explained this in your letter to the Galatians."

"Yes, I wrote,

> The promises were made to Abraham and to his offspring. It does not say, "And to offsprings," referring to many, but referring to one, "And to your offspring," who is Christ (Galatians 3:16).

"I followed this up by writing:

> In Christ Jesus you are all sons of God, through faith. For as many of you as were baptized into Christ have put on Christ. There is neither Jew nor Greek, there is neither slave nor free, there is no male and female, for you are all one in Christ Jesus. And if you are Christ's,

Foresight

> then you are Abraham's offspring, heirs according to promise (Galatians 3:26-29).

"This all means that God's *covenant* with Abraham is fulfilled in the *remnant*—those who believe in Christ—and those who do not believe have been broken off."

Aristarchus replied, "As I remember, James focused on the idea of the *remnant* and recognized that it applies to mankind in general when he addressed the church council at Jerusalem about accepting the Gentiles into the church. He referenced the prophets who declared that God said:

> After this I will return and I will rebuild the tent of David that has fallen; I will rebuild its ruins, and I will restore it, that the *remnant* of mankind may seek the Lord, and all the Gentiles who are called by my name, says the Lord, who makes these things known from of old (Acts 15:15-17).

So evidently God foresaw that the *remnant* of the original *covenant* made with Abraham would eventually come from all mankind."

"You are right on, Brother Aristarchus. Ultimately, the *remnant*, the people of God's *covenant* tree—the *covenant* made with Abraham—are those who believe in Jesus and trust him for salvation. According to his *foreknowledge* of who would choose him, he *predestinated* them to be conformed to the image of Christ.[61] The born-again believers are the *remnant*. They are recipients of the promise:

> "I will bless those who bless you, and him who dishonors you I will curse, and in you all the families of the earth shall be blessed" (Genesis 12:3).

"Then are the Hebrews—the natural offspring of Abraham—who don't believe, without hope? They are without hope outside of Christ, but I believe God has a plan to someday bring them back to

---

[61] See Romans 8:29

himself. Someday, many of them will be awakened to the reality that the Messiah they wait for is Jesus after all. What a great awakening and revival that will be!" declared Paul with a wistful, longing gleam in his eyes.

"But the whole *remnant of all mankind* are heirs to the promise 'I will bless those who bless you, and him who dishonors you I will curse, and in you all the families of the earth shall be blessed.'"

"Do I understand correctly," Brother Paul?"

"Yes indeed, the *remnant* of the *covenant* was originally made up of mostly Abraham's offspring, but the remnant was never exclusively Abraham's offspring. Gentiles could become Jews in the Old Testament and enter God's *covenant.*"

One more question. "We celebrate Christ crucified. We know his death and resurrection provides our salvation, but why did he have to die to save us?"

There are three reasons:
1. Jesus was God so his blood was precarious enough to atone for the whole world. If he had only been man, his blood would only have had enough value to justly save one man. Of course even then God would have had to approve of such an arrangement, which he didn't.
2. He was man so he could die in man's place. The promise was that man would die for his sin. Therefore Jesus had to be man to take man's place.
3. He was sinless so he could die for the sins of others. If he had not been sinless, his death would have involved punishment for his own sin. And he would not have had the pure righteousness to impute to others for their salvation.

Suddenly, the door burst open. A Roman guard entered. "You Paul, have exactly two hours until your time. I suggest you write your final words. Your friend may want to have them."

Just as abruptly as he came, he left.

Foresight

Tears flowed down Aristarchus's face. "Oh, my brother. Has it come to this?"

"Yes, Aristarchus. I only grieve for you. I am ready. I already have my last words written. I have penned them in my second epistle to Timothy for you to take to him:

> I have fought the good fight, I have finished the race, and I have kept the faith. Henceforth there is laid up for me the crown of righteousness, which the Lord, the righteous judge, will award to me on that day, and not only to me but also to all who have loved his appearing (2 Timothy 4:6-8).

"Do not break my heart with your tears, Aristarchus. Try to congratulate me for my entrance into heaven which is about to happen."

Chapter 27

Apostle John and Gaius

"Greetings, Gaius. It is so good to see you have come. I always enjoy our fellowship so much when we have an opportunity to be together."

"You know I feel the same way," replied Gaius. "You always inspire me to love Jesus more because you love him so much. I feel Jesus so near when we talk about him and his love for us and the lost. In fact, today I want to hear some insights from you about the nature of the love Jesus demonstrated. You have been known as the disciple Jesus loved.[62] And Christ's love has shown through you with unusual intensity."

"Well, let's start with a definition. Godly love is God's nature made known in Christ. We come to know this love through observing Jesus as he lives out godly love—the very nature of God. God is love. From Christ's life we understand godly love to be God-centered, unselfish, unlimited, and available to everyone. It loves righteousness and hates wickedness.

---

[62] John 13:23

Foresight

"We cannot claim to know and love God if we break the *covenant* by deliberately walking away from God. But we Christians naturally love God in response to knowing that God first loved us, as I have written.[63] In addition, the Holy Spirit pours out God's love in our hearts.[64] This love rises above mere human love. Therefore, all Christians experience love. We do not force ourselves to love, but we need to keep in close fellowship with the Lord to maintain our first love."

"And this love calls us to worship our Lord together, right?"

"Oh yes, Brother Gaius, God's love calls us to express it and nurture it in fellowship of God with his people. In fact, his love is most effectively developed collectively. As we worship the Lord, together, our love for him grows and we become more conscious of his love toward us as a body. This is why Paul wrote to the Hebrews saying we should not be

> neglecting to meet together, as is the habit of some, but encouraging one another, and all the more as you see the Day drawing near (Hebrews 10:25).

"I hear you loud and clear, Brother John, but I must say I do enjoy getting away from everyone by going up onto a mountain some place and being alone with God to fellowship with him under his blue sky."

"Oh yes, Jesus did this. You remember he went up onto a mountain to pray all night before he chose his disciples. Jesus also said we should go to our room and pray in secret.[65] But this doesn't mean we don't also need the fellowship of God's people. Furthermore, the world needs to see our fellowship and love. You remember I wrote in the gospel of John that Jesus said,

---

[63] 1 John 4:19
[64] Romans 5:5
[65] Matthew 6:6

"By this all people will know that you are my disciples, if you have love for one another" (John 13:25).

"Would you say that love also calls us to keep God's commandments? I believe you have strongly emphasized this in your epistles?"

"Yes, love is basic to keeping Christ's commandments which include the Ten Commandments."

"Oh yes, Brother John. You wrote:

Everyone who makes a practice of sinning also practices lawlessness; sin is lawlessness (1 John 3:4).

You also wrote:

Whoever makes a practice of sinning is of the devil, for the devil has been sinning from the beginning. The reason the Son of God appeared was to destroy the works of the devil. No one born of God makes a practice of sinning, for God's seed abides in him; and he cannot keep on sinning, because he has been born of God (1 John 3:8-9).

I take this to mean that God's seed is love and this love causes us to love God too much to displease him by sinning willfully."

"Yes, Gaius. Anyone who receives God's love and loves God in return will not displease God by doing what he hates. He will not love the world as I wrote in my first epistle:

Do not love the world or the things in the world. If anyone loves the world, the love of the Father is not in him. For all that is in the world—the lust of the flesh, the lust of the eyes, and the pride of life—is not of the Father but is of the world. And the world is passing away, and the lust of it; but he who does the will of God abides forever (1 John 2:16-17).

Loving God turns us away from loving the world and having the lusts the world perpetuates. We no longer live just to pleasure our senses instead living in the joy of the Lord through prayer, study of God's word, and fellowship with our Lord."

Foresight

"Please tell me what you mean by the world. We are in this world. How can we keep from being worldly? We all have to navigate the world through our five senses. We see, hear, smell, taste, and feel the elements of the world. If we didn't, we couldn't even function to fellowship with God and others in developing a spiritual, love relationship with them."

"Oh yes. You have staked out the issue quite well. The world in the context of which I spoke is all that tries to operate apart from God and often in direct opposition to God. And this acting out happens through the three avenues of the world's perverted depravity which I refer to as "all that is in the world" in the passage I just quoted from my first epistle.

"The Lord wants us to enjoy the natural world and function well in it. But to be preoccupied with the earthly and the sensory is to become materialistic and sensual. We must stay close to the Lord and cultivate our love fellowship with him. Love is the key. This is why Jesus taught us that the most important commandment of all in quoting the Old Testament:

> "you shall love the Lord your God with all your heart and with all your soul and with all your mind and with all your strength" (Mark 12:30).

John continued, "As Christians we have a covenant relationship with Jesus, a kind of marriage covenant rooted in godly love. Satan is fiercely jealous of this and the awesome fellowship with God it brings. He tries to seduce us away from the Lord by tempting us with sinful pleasure like he did Eve. He tries to get us to live for the pleasure of gratifying our senses to divert us from worshiping God and developing our spirits to do so. He want us to be '*lovers of pleasure* rather than *lovers of God*' as I wrote to Timothy (2 Timothy 3:4). Being lovers of pleasure is yielding to lust-of-the-flesh sensualism of the world.

"This sensualism is lived out in what appeals to our eyes, the lust-of-the-eyes *materialism*. The spirit of materialism makes us greedy after things and places our *hope* in them instead spiritual riches.

"Sensualism is also lived out in pridefully depending on our own understanding to determine what is right and wrong/good for us and bad for us. This *humanism* makes us inordinately self-dependent instead of placing *faith* in God and his wisdom."

John continued his teaching, "We need to give heed to Paul's instructions in Galatians:"

> Walk in the Spirit, and you shall not fulfill the lust of the flesh. For the flesh lusts against the Spirit, and the Spirit against the flesh; and these are contrary to one another, so that you do not do the things that you wish. But if you are led by the Spirit, you are not under the law. Now the works of the flesh are evident, which are, adultery, fornication, uncleanness, lewdness, idolatry, sorcery, hatred, contentions, jealousies, outbursts of wrath, selfish ambitions, dissensions, heresies, envy, murders, drunkenness, revelries, and the like; of which I tell you beforehand, just as I also told *you* in time past, that those who practice such things will not inherit the kingdom of God.
>
> But the fruit of the Spirit is love, joy, peace, longsuffering, kindness, goodness, faithfulness, gentleness, self-control. Against such there is no law. And those *who are* Christ's have crucified the flesh with its passions and desires. If we live in the Spirit, let us also walk in the Spirit. Let us not become conceited, provoking one another, envying one another (Galatians 5:16-26 NKJV).

"Walking in the Spirit gives life purpose and meaning, filled with the joy of the Lord and freedom from the bondage of sin. Walking in the Spirit *identifies us with Christ's operation to save the lost and conquer the kingdom of the world* instead of loving the world. But

Foresight

living in the lust of the flesh—with the lust of the eyes and the pride of life it incorporates—destroys life and drives us to *despair*."

"Thank you, Brother John. As always, conversation with you is immensely profitable. It has warmed my heart with godly love as never before. Oh how I love my Savior!"

The Roman guards rushed into the room and proceeded to bind John. "We have orders to exile you to the Island of Patmos."

"Oh no!" cried Gaius. "Will you bind me also and take me with John?"

"Absolutely not. We will not have you two colluding against the Empire of Rome."

"God be with you, bless you and keep you, Brother Gaius," said John.

"And God protect you and be with you and bring you back to us," cried Gaius as he thrust out his hands toward John.

"That is enough talk about your God. Don't you know he is the one who has gotten you into all this trouble?"

Chapter 28

Conquest

This chapter is written in a different genre than the rest of this book. The proceeding chapters create imaginary episodes to show the spiritual dynamics in play. This chapter departs from such and attempts to interpret the metaphors and scenarios of the Book of Revelation with exegetical explanations.

John is on the Island called Patmos for the *"word of God and the testimony of Jesus."*[66] In other words, he has been proclaiming what the word of God promises concerning the Messiah and then proclaiming Jesus to be the fulfillment of this Word. These two proclamations are witnesses for God to the world. And these two witnesses are akin to the two "anointed ones" Zechariah saw long ago as two olive trees feeding oil to lampstands for light (Zechariah 4). Remember those two "anointed ones" were the word-of-God proclamation that the temple would be rebuilt and the testimony to the fact that the temple was being built in fulfillment of the word of God.

---

[66] Revelation 1:9 - partial quote of verse

Foresight

John will view these two witnesses in the vision he is about to see, personified as two prophets who stand before the Lord. They are the New Testament "anointed ones." And John will see that the Christians have "conquered by these two witnesses: by the blood of the Lamb and by the word of their testimony" (Revelation 12:11). Yes, they will have believed in the *word* of salvation proclaimed in the blood of the Lamb and will have testified to the fulfilment of this *word* in their lives.

Christians should understand that witnessing in these two ways is God's main assignment to them. Jesus gave the great commission of preaching the gospel-word to his disciples before he ascended to heaven, "Go into all the world and proclaim the gospel to the whole creation" (Mark 16:15). God's word is living and active, accompanied by the convicting power of the Holy Spirit. The gospel-word is key to saving the lost and changing the world. The Bible is God's written word to the world. It becomes his living and active Word as people receive it *unfolded* by the Holy Spirit into their hearts and minds and proclaim it to others.

John has set the example for the followers of Christ by preaching the Word and its fulfilment. This has provoked the enemies of Jesus to exile him to Patmos, but here again God is going to use the act of the enemy to further his cause. Here in Patmos John will receive the necessary revelation to encourage God's people to conquer under all circumstances.

John is about to receive the word of God concerning the future. This word is a revelation of Jesus Christ specifically addressed to the seven churches of Asia Minor and generally to all churches of all times. But it is not directed to the world. It is directed to the Church of Jesus Christ.

The seven churches of Asia Minor and Christendom at large can no longer be complacent, because the espionage of Satan has been infiltrating the churches. The spirit of indifference has cooled once fervent love of God. The spirituality of relationship with God is threatened with non-spiritual legalism. Balaam-like self-centered corruption is attempting to turn the gospel into money-making schemes. The Nicolaitans are spreading the idea that God doesn't care if people commit fornication and other sins of the flesh. Others claim to have secret knowledge so people will come to them for instruction instead of following the apostles. Besides all of this drama within, wicked forces without are arising with intent to kill God's people and stamp out the gospel message.

In light of these happenings, Revelation calls the Christians to "conquer"[67] whatever keeps them from being on fire for God and a powerful impact on society. Such conquests will become part of Christ's larger operation to save the lost and conquer the kingdom of this world. And at this point in time, the dedication to Christ's operation involves willingness to accept martyrdom.

The saints are to develop martyr's hearts, realizing that martyrdom plays a huge part in advancing God's kingdom. But they are not to be discouraged by this. They are to discover the awesome joy afforded those who achieve a martyr's level of commitment. Whoever conquers through martyrdom will be highly rewarded. God has a special place in his heart for his martyrs. And the time is near:

> "Blessed is the one who reads aloud the words of this prophecy, and blessed are those who hear, and who keep what is written in it, for the time is near" (1:3).

• • •

The time is near. What can this mean? The book of Revelation tells of events to happen over 2,000 years hence. So this cannot mean that all the events it tells of are near. On the other hand, it is absurd

---

[67] All seven churches are challenged to "conquer" (chapters 2 and 3). Some other versions say "overcome."

Foresight

to suggest—as some have—that it is only near in God's timing. They say one day is as a thousand years in God's timing, so the happenings are near even if they are thousands of years away. This makes no sense. The message is not intended to communicate to God. It is intended to communicate to people.

The only explanation that makes any sense is that the inauguration of God's coming operation—as will be described—is near. The inauguration is near. A more advanced *operation to save the lost and conquer the kingdom of this world* will soon to be inaugurated.

Upon its inauguration, what some theologians call the *already but not yet,* will be in play. Even though a more advanced operation will be in place at the point of inauguration, the operation will not be in its final stage. Then at various points in the future, what has *not yet* been in operation will arrive in a more advanced stage than *already* had been in operation. Eventually this operation of his kingdom by his army, the church, will bring the kingdom to its final stage when the creation itself will be set free from its bondage to corruption and obtain the freedom of the glory of the children of God (Romans 8:21).

The book of Revelation shows the kingdom of God marching forward through all the hell, hate, and martyrdom Satan throws at it. All readers who identify with this march will have their hearts inspired by a sense of victory and winning. They will be challenged to a high level of commitment. And as they develop martyr's hearts in the process, they will come forth with powerful passion to serve their crucified Lord at all costs.

. . .

John sees the Son of Man with seven stars in his right hand, walking among seven lampstands. Jesus explains the mystery of the

Conquest

stars and lampstands: the stars are angels and the lampstands are the churches. So right from the start, the vision is in symbols.

This is a strong clue that the Book of Revelation contains symbols and metaphors which cannot be taken literally. The Old Testament prophets communicated spiritual truths in metaphors and Jesus taught in parables. Revelation does the same. The symbols are not to be taken literally.

Who would think that Zechariah's vision of Joshua's filthy garments was about teaching Joshua to take a bath and wash his clothes? Was the prophet's vision of women with wings about teaching women to fly? Was his vision about oil being piped to a lampstand from olive trees to be taken literally? Was the vision showing people to pipe oil directly from olive trees to the lampstand in the temple? Who would suggest that the parable of the sower was intended to teach a farmer how to plant and grow crops? Yet the modern trend of interpretation, often called dispensational eschatology, insists the book of Revelation must be interpreted literally.

John will see multifaceted, colorful metaphors, many of which have already been set forth by the Old Testament prophets. These metaphors beg to be interpreted with spiritual foresight and insight.

• • •

John sees one seated on the throne with a scroll of destiny in his hand, but no one is found worthy to open it. John begins to weep, thinking he will not get to see what is to come after all. But then it is found that

> "the Lion of the tribe of Judah, the Root of David, has conquered, so that he can open the scroll and its seven seals" (5:5).

But now the Lion, seen as a Lamb who has been slain, approaches the throne. He takes the scroll out of the hand of him who

Foresight

is seated on the throne. As the Lamb, he made the sufficient sin offering:
>   1. Jesus was God so his blood was precarious enough to die for the whole world.
>   2. He was man so he could die in man's place.
>   3. He was sinless so he could die for the sins of others.

This gives him power to conquer as the Lion. The conquest he has made on the cross has bought the victory needed for all Christians to have the power they will need to conquer the challenges yet to be revealed in the scroll. Up until the calvary victory, Satan had most people intimidated into believing they could not have full deliverance from sin's bondage. But now they live in the faith of sins forgiven and hearts cleansed. They have faith in in the blood of the Lamb, this faith that is strengthened by their testimony.[68] On this foundation, they have the faith, love, and hope to conquer the challenges ahead, even as martyrs if necessary.

Yes. The Lamb is seen to be the only one worthy to open the scroll revealing the future, winning operation. He has conquered by his death, so he is worth to open the future to those who will be called to conquer in this future as martyrs, if necessary. Furthermore, his death *for* sin has given them power to die *to* sin. No wonder the twenty-four elders in heaven, who have already conquered, are enraptured and begin to sing and rejoice:

> "Worthy are you to take the scroll and to open its seals, for you were slain, and by your blood you ransomed people for God from every tribe and language and people and nation, and you have made them a kingdom and priests to our God, and they shall reign on the earth" (5:9-10).

---

[68] See Revelation 12:11

The elders are enraptured with the joy of having been ransomed. And this salvation is so awesome to them that they are thrilled to identify with the cause of bringing it to others.

The Lamb prepared to open the scroll (chapter 6). And with this, the Lord's operation to change the course of history is about to be *inaugurated*. The Lamb begins to pull the seals off the scroll. The seals are a *preface* of what is to come. What is to come does not happen in the opening of the seals, for the scroll of destiny cannot unroll as long as the seals are binding it from unrolling. But in the seals, the reader can get a general preview of what is to come.

The Lamb pulls the first seal loose. A *white horse* (the kingdom of God) mounted by a crowned rider (Jesus) accepts an archer's bow and comes forth conquering and to conquer. This horse and rider set the stage: the kingdom of God's militant operation to conquer the kingdom of this world will begin as soon as the scroll begins to unroll.[69]

The second seal is removed. A bright *red horse* (war) charges forward as its rider grabs the handle of the sword held out to him. The rider (a tyrant) is impatient to draw blood and take peace from the earth.

The third seal reveals a *black steed* (financial crash) mounted by a man with scales in his hand (famine). He wreaks havoc on the economy until the scales weigh out only two pounds of wheat or six pounds of barley in exchange for a whole day's wages. The price of oil and wine is too costly for anyone.

The fourth seal brings a *pale horse* (death) high stepping on to the scene with a rider (sin) who is single-mindedly focused on fighting God. He destroys lives by the sword, famine, pestilence, and wild beasts.

---

[69] See Revelation 11:15

Foresight

As is seen in Zechariah's visions, the *colored horses* are God's providence at work. However, in the Holy Spirit dispensation there is a distinct difference. God still manipulates the evil designs of the enemy (which cause famine, war, and death) as one means to keep his agenda on track as the last three of the four horses show. But the white horse—being the kingdom ruled by Jesus in the person of the Holy Spirit—is present in a way he was not in the Old Testament. He rules from the throne of godly hearts over his kingdom, now present in society. The kingdom no longer rules from a distance as in the Old Testament.

This means God's strategy is different in the New Testament dispensation. God is not as quick to use another nation to bring judgment on an evil nation as he was prone to do in the Old Testament. And God is not as quick to bring some other kind of judgment. God's kingdom is designed to bring deliverance from evil through the gospel.

But for the pessimists, they see the wickedness of society as creating a hopeless situation. They are more inclined to despair than to hope. Of course the king of despair is happy to help them *despair*. Satan is happy to help them think the wickedness means the end of time is near and only Christ's physical return can correct the situation. The devil would never want them to expect a spiritual move of God to change the situation.

Jesus is riding forth as the kingdom-of-God conqueror in the person of the Holy Spirit to convict the world of sin, righteousness, and judgment. This makes the difference. God's people can expect the Holy Spirit to bring awakening as they pray and do their part to spread the gospel. It is a major trick of the devil to give Christians the idea that the only thing God-loving people should expect is judgment on society instead of awakening and revival.

Those who *identify with Christ's operation to save the lost and conquer the kingdom of the world* find their joy and fulfillment in this identity. They have greater confidence in the power of the Gospel than those who fail to embrace this identity. Those who identify tend to focus more on praying and working for a great awakening with a great expectancy. They have a stronger passion to disciple young Christians because they envision a greater, more long-term future. They have a strong sense of being a part of a winning cause here and now, and the more they project this, the more others want to join the cause.

God is showing John that he still works through the evil designs of the enemy as one means of keeping God's agenda on track when he sees fit. This will be shown in the three remaining seals needing to be removed in order for the scroll to begin to unroll its *revelation.*

To appreciate what is being revealed, one has to see Almighty God as sovereign Lord over the life of all nature and all creatures. He acts directly to produce good. He also acts works through the evil intents of evil people to produce good. Furthermore, he acts to reward the righteous and bring judgment on the wicked. These various kinds of acts are revealed throughout John's vision.

Those who refuse to worship God as sovereign Lord and recognize his right to act as he sees fit will be in constant turmoil. They will be fighting what they cannot change, and if they take it on themselves to charge God with injustice, they will face his judgment. The sooner people rest in God's wisdom for what he causes or allows to happen, the sooner they will find peace.

All of the Lord's acts to keep his agenda on track bring good to those who love and serve him as he promises (see Romans 8:28) But he doesn't promise to save them from all adversity.

The Lamb opens the fifth seal and John saw

under the altar the souls of those who had been slain for the *word of God and for the witness* they had borne. They cried out with a loud voice, "O Sovereign Lord, holy and true, how long before you will

Foresight

> judge and avenge our blood on those who dwell on the earth?" (6:9-10).

The martyred souls are told to rest a little longer, until the others are killed. Many more will die for their faith before the *kingdom of God finally conquers the kingdom of this world.* (See Revelation 11:15). When the right time comes, their blood will be avenged in a powerful way. The heavenly Father does not take their killing lightly, but he allows his saints to die for their faith to advance his cause. The blood of such martyrs is destined to become the seed of the church.

• • •

The first readers of John's book who discerned they might soon face martyrdom did not have to view themselves as *victims*. Rather they were intended to view themselves as *victors,* as extremely important soldiers in *Christ's operation to save the lost and conquer the kingdom of the world.* The more the devil would kill the saints, the more the church would grow. This understanding would keep the Christians from the otherwise potential *despair*, what Satan was striving for.

• • •

The sixth seal opens to a great earthquake. The sun is black. The full moon is like blood, and the stars fall to the earth like figs blown to the ground by a gale. The sky rolls up like a scroll, and every mountain and island shifts to a new location. This picture shows God finally destroying the environment which gave people the opportunity to serve God as he brings them to a final judgement.

All the wicked hide in caves, calling to the mountains and rocks:

> "Fall on us and hide us from the face of him who is seated on the throne, and from the wrath of the Lamb, for the great day of their wrath has come, and who can stand?" (6:15-17).

Conquest

There is absolutely no mercy left for those who have had the power to act with the Lord instead of against him. Those who have martyred the believers have the greatest reason to fear.

Now 144,000 from all twelve tribes of Israel (all the servants of God on earth) are sealed. This is to protect them from the calamities which are to come from the four winds of the earth. The winds of nature are the result of uneven temperatures in conflict. Thus, the winds of the earth metaphorically depict people in conflict with what is good for them. They fight themselves through their own sin. This blows havoc into individual lives and into society as a whole.

The angels holding back the winds depict protection from society's sins and sin's effects. The Holy Spirit seals his people by setting them apart from society's sins. This protects them from the destructive winds those sins cause. God's people love God and their neighbors as themselves. They don't hate, steal, and murder. They don't tell deliberate lies. They don't lust after one another's spouses. They don't get drunk. They don't take mind-altering drugs and do other self-destructive things. They live separately from sinful practices.

These servants of the Lord assemble together to worship and celebrate the God of their salvation. They make time for prayer and Bible study. Generally speaking, they live godly lives and this holiness is their seal from the destructive winds of wicked living.

The sealing of the saints must also include God's overt actions to directly protect them because they are righteous. For example, God saved Noah and his family by putting them in the ark. This was additional protection beyond the direct protection their righteous living gave them.

John's vision now turns from the saints on earth, to those who have graduated from the tribulation they experienced on earth to their reward in heaven:

Foresight

> They are before the throne of God and serve him day and night in his temple; and he who sits on the throne will shelter them with his presence. They shall hunger no more, neither thirst anymore; the sun shall not strike them, nor any scorching heat. For the Lamb in the midst of the throne will be their shepherd, and he will guide them to springs of living water, and God will wipe away every tear from their eyes (7:15-17).

In the presence of these saints, the Lamb opens the seventh seal to reveal seven angels holding trumpets (chapter 8). Another angel pours incense (God's will), along with the prayers of the earthly saints, on the fire burning on the altar. The incense (God's will) mingled with the prayers of his saints (the smoke rising from the incense) shows how they are praying in harmony with his will. Another angel takes the fire (the Holy Spirit-anointed prayers) from the altar with his censer and hurls it to the earth. This judgmental fire of seven plagues will check evil powers and prevent them from destroying his sovereign agenda.

Notice God works in conjunction with the prayers of his people. They do not command him with their prayers. The Holy Spirit reveals God's will to those who pray so they can be praying in his will. They pray in the context of, "Your kingdom come, your will be done, on earth as it is in heaven" (Matthew 6:10).

This further *identifies them with Christ's operation to save the lost and conquer the kingdom of the world.* They develop a passion to pray for a great world-wide spiritual awakening. They pray passionately together for this until they are effectively interceding in prayer. The smoke of their collective, fervent prayer-agreement is blended with the will-of-God incense to move him to continue to free the creation from its bondage as Paul wrote to the Romans (Romans 8:19-21). In this case, it comes in the form of corrective, judgmental fire.

Conquest

All that is revealed as the scroll unrolls the future leads to the time when:

> The kingdom of the world has become the kingdom of our Lord and of his Christ, and he shall reign forever and forever (Revelation 11:13).

The kingdom of God, the stone cut from a mountain, continues its advance on the kingdom of Satan, the kingdom of this world. And with it, Jesus is building his Church in spite of what all the gates of hell do prevail against it. In other words, these gates cannot hold back the gospel from winning the lost. Neither can the ole devil with all of his kingdom forces prevail against the onslaught of the kingdom of God conquering his kingdom. Christ's operation through his army, the church, is on the march *to win the lost and conquer the kingdom of his world.*

> For the creation waits with eager longing for the revealing of the sons of God. For the creation was subjected to futility, not willingly, but because of him who subjected it, in hope that the creation itself will be set free from its bondage to corruption and obtain the freedom of the glory of the children of God. For we know that the whole creation has been groaning together in the pains of childbirth until now. And not only the creation, but we ourselves, who have the firstfruits of the Spirit, groan inwardly as we wait eagerly for adoption as sons, the redemption of our bodies. For in this hope we were saved. Now hope that is seen is not hope. For who hopes for what he sees? But if we hope for what we do not see, we wait for it with patience (Romans 8:19-25).

A future book will be forthcoming to interpret the rest of the book of revelation.

Final Thoughts

The Bible is God's written word to us. As we receive it *unfolded* by the Holy Spirit into our hearts and minds and proclaim it to others, it becomes God's living and active word. Yes, we cannot just receive it, for it to be living and active, we must also proclaim it to others for it be fully living and active. Throughout the Bible, the expressions: "God's word", "the word of God", and "the word of the Lord" usually refer to the communicated word of God, not the uncommunicated written word of God. The written word is often referred to as "the Scripture" or "the Scriptures."

The idea of God's word "living and active" in us should spark fire in our bones. This idea should give us a passion to be a part of receiving and proclaiming the Bible—the inerrant, *written word of the Lord*. And as we follow through on this, we will be ablaze for God with continually growing faith, love, and hope.

www.ingramcontent.com/pod-product-compliance
Lightning Source LLC
Chambersburg PA
CBHW070547050426
42450CB00011B/2756